**Reinventing
Texas Government**

Reinventing Texas Government

Michael Lauderdale

 UNIVERSITY OF TEXAS PRESS, AUSTIN

First edition, 1999

Requests for permission to reproduce material from this
work should be sent to Permissions, University of Texas Press,
Box 7819, Austin, TX 78713-7819.

♾ The paper used in this book meets the minimum
requirements of ANSI / NISO Z39.48-1992 (R1997)
(Permanence of Paper).

LIBRARY OF CONGRESS CATALOGING-IN-PUBLICATION DATA

Lauderdale, Michael L.
Reinventing Texas government / Michael Lauderdale. —
1st ed.
        p.   cm.
Includes bibliographical references and index.
ISBN 0-292-74711-X (pbk. : alk. paper)
1. Texas — Politics and government — 1951–
2. Organizational effectiveness.   3. Organizational
effectiveness — Evaluation.   4. Organizational change —
Evaluation.   I. Title.
JK4841.L38   1999
352.3'67'09794 — ddc21

                                        98-25509

To those who use and have helped develop the Survey of Organizational Excellence and to their efforts to create organizations

Contents

| Acknowledgments

This book and the related activities of the survey have benefited from numerous contributions. Many of the ideas began to germinate through my work with dozens of small community groups, self-help organizations, and small businesses in the 1960s. Over the years I have had the additional opportunity to work with a number of large businesses, especially the Prudential Insurance Company, 3M, and IBM, where a number of the concerns for quality expressed in this book were first articulated. Then through the encouragement of Barbara White and with the leadership of Albert Hawkins and John Barton, we created a tool and companion effort that continues to grow.

Since 1995 Shannon Gilliland has been a tireless contributor, coordinating the survey effort and making hundreds of presentations to participating organizations, students, and professional meetings. She has led the effort to increase the flexibility of the survey, grinding through thousands of lines of code so that results could be quickly returned and with hundreds of variations. She wrote much of the initial versions of the material that appears in Chapters 2 and 3 and has spurred efforts to use the survey data in concerted organizational change.

Michael Kelly of the University of Missouri has been my collaborator for twenty-five years, working with me in the 1970s and with many of the survey participants today. He has pioneered applying the survey to organizations in other states and annually teaches with me a graduate course that is largely based on a World Wide Web version of the survey. Michael continues to lead the way to convert the survey effort to pedagogical concepts and techniques for use in the university classroom and organizational training settings.

Leadership from the State of Texas and its agencies were significant sources in strengthening the survey. Governor Richards strongly endorsed extending the survey to more state agencies. Governor Bush challenged us to involve all state agencies and every state employee. He has brought to the survey effort leadership that respects every employee and a call for choosing only the most important things and then doing them well. In November 1997, he called all heads of state agencies and the chairmen of boards and commissions to endorse survey efforts and reiterate his call for excellence in state government.

Albert Hawkins of the Legislative Budget Office in 1995 and then as the director of the Governor's Office of Budget and Planning in 1995 and 1996 worked with us unstintingly to adapt procedures and findings to the needs of agencies, the Legislature, and the state's executive offices. Mr. Hawkins regularly reviewed data and narrative reports and provided encouragement to state agencies to promote higher levels of attainment. Albert continues to provide immeasurably important commentary and thoughtfulness in focusing efforts to make material readily usable by agencies and by executive and legislative offices. We have been particularly fortunate to have the additional assistance of Dr. Edward Baldwin of those offices in keeping the survey abreast of other initiatives in state government. Similarly, Ara Marjanian directed our work and attention to the efforts by the state to secure customer satisfaction measures as part of agencies' strategic plans.

John Barton of the Legislative Budget Board helped us develop procedures for adapting findings so that agencies could use survey data in biennial strategic plans and appropriations requests. John has kept us mindful of how survey data can be used in strategic planning, and he maintained liaison with leaders in the State Legislature, especially Representative Henry Cuellar and Representative Rob Junell. Mr. Junell, the chairman of the House Appropriations Committee, and Janis Carter, clerk of the House Appropriations Committee, provided important opportunities to relate survey data to the deliberations of the Appropriations Committee.

Morris Winn of the Texas Department of Insurance, Jeannie Weaver of the Texas Department of Health, Patricia Vistein and Dave

Gustafson of the Texas Workforce Commission, Eric Young of the Texas Youth Commission, and Mark Majek of the State Board of Nurse Examiners contributed important ideas on the use of the survey in their organizations. Brian Francis and Bill Kuntz made an early "acid test" of the constructs and helped me to understand more clearly the relationships between description of organizational conditions and the selection of interventions. Barry Bales of the LBJ School of Public Affairs has been the source of numerous discussions on the role of training to build stronger organizations and the need for legislative involvement in the efforts of state agencies to improve.

Many of my graduate students have played significant roles in extending survey concepts. Tricia Shircliff coordinated agency contacts with the 1994 survey; Terry Ware helped get the 1996 data set adapted to later versions of software applications; Lee Gustafson did many of the early graphic conversions of text to the Web; and Troy Griggsby single-handedly coded the first HTML version of the survey and built our original Web site. Noel Landuyt worked with the first Web version of the survey used by the University of Texas at Austin's Applied Research Laboratories. Noel continues as a leader in promoting the survey to higher education.

Many colleagues provided comments and helped set an atmosphere that made the development of this book more thought-provoking. Katherine Selber, Cal Streeter, Richard W. Hendrickson, Don Blashill, Guy E. Shuttlesworth, Bill Lasher, Kay Franklin, Kelley Jones, George Herbert, and Pat Lauderdale were the source of countless discussions of theory and empirical studies dealing with quality, organizational change, and the application of commercial concepts to government. Over the last twenty years close friends have brought us back repeatedly to challenges faced in human resources as the world grows more interconnected and markets become global. Robert Black of the Prudential Company, Norman Chenven, M.D., of the Austin Regional Clinic, Ted Pickens, Merle Ackerman, and Bill McLellan of 3M, Tom Backus, Keith Brewer, and John Hannifan of IBM, Jim Schwab of General Electric, and William Swanson of St. Francis Associates have provided opportunities for research and application of ideas presented in the survey. They have, moreover, been great and supportive critics of academic notions as we have sought to apply theory to rapidly changing markets and fiercely competitive arenas.

Ruth McRoy, Fran Danis, Paul White, Harriet Sullivan, John Trapp, and other staff of the Center for Social Work Research as well as staff of the School of Social Work, but particularly Julie Cunniff and Kelly Larson, provided a variety of support on purchasing, vouchering, software applications, and reliably directing user inquiries about the survey. Students in my classes here and those in Professor Kelly's at the University of Missouri at Columbia over the years have contributed much in making these materials readable to persons new to survey concepts and organizational development.

I have been especially fortunate to have an exceptional working relationship with the University of Texas Press. My editor, science editor Shannon Davies, has been both a source of constant encouragement and an important arbiter of style and idiom necessary to shape a manuscript that must be responsive to many different audiences. The Press's managing editor, Carolyn Wylie, has contributed tirelessly in searching for innumerable errors and helping keep a focus upon the manuscript during busy days.

Lastly, I want to pay special thanks to my collaborator and academic dean, Barbara W. White. Barbara's continual willingness to provide leadership for these efforts in our own university and her own unflagging devotion to equality and efforts that embody relevance to the crucial issues of today make this endeavor especially rewarding.

Michael Lauderdale
Austin, Texas
July 1998

Introduction
Change in Texas

On a bright and sunny day in April 1995, I walked south from my campus office for a few blocks to a meeting scheduled at the Governor's Offices at the Texas Capitol. The rains had been generous that spring, and a stand of Texas bluebonnets was still in full glory along my walk, reminding all visitors of those days when the broad prairie and longhorn cattle were much the world of Texas. The red granite stone of the Capitol and the live oaks provided a background of tranquillity and the sense of history important to the central structures of every government.

Some of the governor's senior staff members had set this meeting back in March to identify and examine procedures to assess customer satisfaction with services from state government. The meeting happened to fall on Thursday, April 20, the day after the bombing of the Alfred P. Murrah Federal Building in Oklahoma City 400 miles to the north of Austin. As I walked across the Capitol grounds, I saw more uniformed state and Capitol police and rangers on the grounds and in every building than I had ever seen before. As I passed many of the officers, their faces were grave and uneasy and their voices betrayed tenseness. Such behavior was unusual, as duty at the Capitol typically has a strong public relations component, and officers are almost invariably easygoing, friendly, and relaxed.

When I arrived at my meeting, I spoke to my host and said, "Albert, I have never seen so many security personnel on the Capitol grounds." Albert replied that this was likely a record number and we both talked briefly about the Oklahoma tragedy. At that point, only twenty-four hours after the bombing, little was known of who had committed the act and there was considerable concern that more blasts could come. The one thing that both Albert and I knew, without making the fear concrete by verbalizing it, was that if it could happen in Oklahoma City, it could happen anywhere, including Austin, Texas. We realized that the Oklahoma City bombing was an ominous challenge and a brutal threat to citizens and their government.

Whatever history may prove about the events of the previous day in Oklahoma—whether the act was that of a single madman or something orchestrated by some larger, shadowy conspiracy—one thing is clear about feelings toward government. Much of government and many governmental organizations are viewed with anger and suspicion from parts of the public. To a substantial degree both national political parties have run in recent years against government on platforms to reform, reinvent, and downsize government. Numerous polls indicate that the public does not hold government or governmental workers in high esteem. Such sentiments seem common all across the United States; yet clearly they are not necessarily the trend in other parts of the world. The significant regard that the English, French, or Japanese citizen holds for civil servants is not enjoyed today by any branch of American government.

Government in the United States always exists only on a franchise from the people. The people exist a priori and then the government is created. The election process is part of the franchise. Less visible yet vital parts of the franchise are the willingness of citizens to perform such civic duties as voting, serving on juries, paying taxes, and doing the countless volunteer tasks that maintain the community. In a small way, the material in this book is about many endeavors by Texas government to ensure that the franchise of the people is not lessened by its agencies from having grown callous, indifferent, irrelevant, and out of touch.

Three different, separate, and yet related sets of information are presented in this book. One is the description of a detailed and involved process underway for several years in Texas that seeks the improvement of state agencies. Chapters 1 and 6 directly address change that is associated with the use of the survey. Persons working in state government in Texas and other states should find this material useful and perhaps familiar. The second set of information in this book is the presentation of a tool for measuring the attitudes of employees in any organization and using that information to strengthen an organization. I have presented in Chapters 3 through 5 a step-by-step explanation of why surveys are useful, how a survey is built and used, and how to return data to the organization. One should conduct a survey not simply to capture the "state of affairs" of the moment but also to provide a foundation for analyses and change. These chapters emphasize how survey data are used to promote positive change. These chapters should be of particular interest to persons in any organization charged with the responsibility of improving organizations. From the perspective of the book, this responsibility should be shared by everyone in the organization, so the material is presented to address all roles in an organization. The third set of material in this book is more historical and wide-ranging and seeks to identify the forces in American society that impel change in all organizations. It attempts to explain why there is today such great emphasis on the need to change and improve public and private organizations and where this push for change is taking us. My effort is to present both a longer and wider view of how all organizations are put together and how, I think, they will need to be changed.

The tool presented in this book, the Survey of Organizational Excellence, is an evolving concept that has been used for nearly two decades in Texas state government. It has now been applied in a variety of organizations, including entities outside Texas government, and with tens of thousands of employees. Findings and conclusions presented in this book represent a continuous process, an ongoing experiment yielding a wealth of quantified data and hundreds of real-life applications of activities to create better organizations.

Briefly, the details of the chapters are as follows. The first chapter provides a history of the development of the Survey of Organizational Excellence. Originally developed as a tool to estimate employee attitudes, it has grown to become a means to assess organizational strengths and increase employee involvement. It is widely used by organizations of Texas state government and provides crucial data upon which to base organizational changes. Chapter 2 explains why such surveys are in general use in many businesses and agencies and how best to conduct a survey in an organization. It includes explanations of why a survey is beneficial and directions for how to distribute a survey, how to answer typical questions from participants, and other practical questions that arise when one conducts a survey. Chapter 3 provides an explicit description of the instrument and the ways in which the data are returned to the organization. Chapter 4 introduces the concept of organizational assessments and shows how the data from the survey can be used to identify possible problems. The chapter provides some interventions appropriate for each type of problem. Chapter 5 offers some attributes that characterize visionary leaders and explains how one returns the data from the survey to members of the organization and involves members in solving identified problems. The chapter is particularly directed to the responsibilities of leadership in using the survey. Gathering survey information from employees implies that the data will be used for the benefit of all. The chapter explains how one can make good on the implied commitment. Chapter 6 presents some of the data gathered over recent years from organizations that use the survey. It illustrates how one can employ the survey to gain a general description of an organization and provides information about the kinds of problem identification that are possible with the survey. Chapter 7 provides details about how and why organizations have changed over the years and what are the most significant challenges organizations and leadership face today. It looks at what assumptions are made about individuals and organizations and how those assumptions affect what the organization does. Chapter 8 critiques the push for quality that demands attention from many organizations and outlines how successful organizations must function today and what future organizations must look like. These last two chapters contain critical information for leadership, providing some of the roadmap into the next century that will be vital to all organizations.

All organizations, public and private, must continually strive to improve the use of resources and increase responsiveness to the environment (i.e., markets, constituents, clients, and competitors). Successful change in any organization requires three elements. One element is *leadership.* Change requires leadership that can envision a mission that will enable the organization to acquire resources and compete successfully in its environment. A successful vision must be a bit of prophecy, an accurate prediction of what product or service will meet current and future needs. Leadership must secure trust with members of the organization and inspire dedication and creativity. The second requisite for successful change is outside (environmental) information for the organization, especially about how clients or customers perceive the goods and services the organization provides. This is simply *external data* important to the organization. Assessing customer satisfaction on a product or service is an example of gathering external data. *Internal data* is the third requisite for successful change. An organization must have some means of pulling together all of the information about processes, individual feelings, organizational conflicts, communication blockages, and so forth that occur within any organization and it must act on that information to permit an organization to grow more capable. The Survey of Organizational Excellence, as presented in this book, is a tool designed expressly for acquiring and distilling meaning about *internal data*. It provides a means of collecting the data, extracting useful information from the findings, and offering leadership a way to use the findings to involve all members of the organization in desired change.

The survey provides *internal data* that captures an in-depth view of the culture of an organization: the attitudes, beliefs, and values held by the people who are at the core of the organization—the employees. It provides a picture of many issues that are important to effective organizational functioning. Research and experience indicate that systematically acquiring employee perceptions is an essential step toward continuous improvement. Those organizations that achieve the highest level of employee dedication and participation will have a head start down the path toward excellence and quality. This document details the application of one indispensable tool to increase employee commitment to the organization.

The process described in this book details the best use of the survey as a vehicle for communication and organizational improvement. Used properly, employee surveys are a tool that can effect significant and positive change in the work environment. The information presented is based on employee survey practices found in the private sector and research literature as well as on insight from employees who have used the tool to improve their organizations. The overall survey process, as detailed in the following pages, points an organization down a path of continuous activity to promote openness, employee accountability, commitment, and dedication to improvement. Gathering of the survey data and using the data to chart steps for improvement are at the core of principles that are articulated in the quality movement across America today. Such processes serve to build the "thinking organizations" suggested in this book; these processes include placing high levels of empowerment, participation, responsibility, and trust in all members of the organization. These "thinking organizations" are, interestingly, quite consonant with many of the founding principles and beliefs of American democracy. They are characteristic of the organizations that are replacing those with industrial, specialized, and large-scale attributes. These "thinking organizations" are also continuous with beliefs in individual striving and civic responsibility central to the special qualities of the American character. Thus, the results from the processes described in this book build both stronger organizations and individuals who are more creative in their work and more capable in responding to family and civic responsibilities beyond the work organization.

**Reinventing
Texas Government**

1 | History and Development of the Survey of Organizational Excellence

The use of surveys to determine employees' feelings, preferences, and attitudes about working in a given organization has been a routine practice for at least four decades. The concept of understanding the importance of what employees think about work gained first momentum in the late 1920s with studies by Roethlisberger and Dickson and other researchers in manufacturing settings influenced by the pioneering work of Elton Mayo.[1] After this important research, workers were seen to bring complex motivations to the work site, and findings from both the immediate work setting and the culture of the factory extended the understanding of factors influencing worker satisfaction and productivity. During and after World War II studies of combat units, resistance groups in Europe during Axis occupation, and the tactics that American prisoners of war used to survive in Japanese concentration camps increased understandings of the role of leadership, team solidarity, and values in various settings.[2] Surveys then added these concepts to the original concerns about working conditions, compensation, and organizational culture.

Pressures in the 1960s to provide a greater inclusion of other groups in the society into business, education, and government moved the use of surveys to many different kinds of organizations. Indeed, since that tumultuous decade, efforts have grown to make organizations more open to people from a variety of backgrounds and increase both creativity and efficiency. The development of the Survey of Organizational Excellence (SOE) is reflective of these forces and clearly rooted both in advances in social science and the broadening activities of the culture to extend the democratic franchise to all.

The SOE itself reflects several trends. One is simply that organizations, and in this case governments, are becoming more creative, effective, and efficient. Dozens of programs in almost all walks of American life are underway to create better organizations. Reengineering and reinventing concepts are common, as are many techniques to speed up processes, increase environmental response rates, and heighten quality. A second trend is the realization that vigorous state government entities are essential to a healthy economy, safe communities, and a citizenry that respects public institutions and, in turn, is well served by those institutions. A third trend is that all organizations, public and private, exist today in a complex and rapidly changing environment that demands the highest levels of adaptability and creativity. This trend has resulted in the call for "learning" or "thinking" organizations. These are organizations highly adept in understanding new conditions and adapting to a new environment. The history of the SOE reflects these trends and illustrates in one state, Texas, how these trends are changing state government, organizations, and the relationships between employees and the organization and the larger community.

How the Survey Began

The SOE had its beginnings in Texas state government in 1979 with a telephone call from the newly elected governor of Texas, William Clements, to the president of the University of Texas at Austin, Peter Flawn. This was an interesting time in Texas. Because of sharply rising oil prices in the 1970s, the state was experiencing rapid growth in population and wealth. Yet many thoughtful leaders in the state were aware of diminishing petroleum reserves and the need for the Texas economy to develop other sources of wealth and opportunities for employment. Leadership at the University of Texas, personalized through President Flawn, saw this as an opportunity to build the kind of research programs that could generate new businesses and jobs. Flawn called upon the university and its backers to commit to an unstinting push to achieve excellence. Flawn, through his presidency, led the university in an unprecedented drive to secure endowments for faculty and programs and to increase the role of the university in programs to incubate new industries. During his administration, the University became the nation's most highly endowed public university, and the ground was laid for outstanding achievement in a number of fields. Among the most striking has been the creation of computer companies that permitted Austin to start to rival Silicon Valley of San Jose, California, and the complex along Route 128 in Boston, Massachusetts.[3] Both the SEMATECH consortium and the Microelectronics and Computer Technology Corporation (MCC) consortium arguably came from this drive and generated the computer hardware and software complex that now exists in Austin.

Governor Clements, like Flawn, was a strong-willed and independent leader. Clements was the first Republican governor elected in Texas since the Civil War and brought to the office different ideas of governing than had been characteristic of many of his predecessors. He held little allegiance to the way things had long been done in state government, since he was neither a product of the dominant and long-ensconced Democratic Party nor an active player in county courthouse and local precinct politics. Such politics have long been the training ground for many elected officials in both the Democratic and Republican parties. The historical pattern during much of the period since the 1940s has been to stress an accommodation to events and an incremental approach to change.

In contrast to officials raised in this process, Clements had a background in running very large organizations. During the Nixon administration he was a deputy secretary of the Department of Defense and was experienced in promulgating and controlling billion-dollar budgets that procured large amounts of weaponry and paid salaries to millions of enlisted and civilian personnel. He had additionally created and run a large oil well service company with international operations. Thus, Clements came to the Governor's Office as a person who understood and had run large entities, businesses, and governmental bureaucracies as well as a capable political campaigner who knew how to win elections.

A Governor's Perspective

Governor Clements wanted to tune and invigorate state government so that it would be a magnet to attract new industry and business to the state. As part of his new administration, he sought to gain some fix on how capable state government was. Thus early in his administration,

Governor Clements asked President Flawn for some names of faculty members who might poll state employees to determine how those persons felt about working for the state. Flawn, in turn, contacted one of his faculty, Martha Williams, whom he later named as the dean of the School of Social Work. Williams had experience in building work teams and doing assessments of organizations. She was also assisting me in a research project that I was doing with the Prudential Insurance Company. That effort examined how Prudential could improve its success in operating relatively new ventures in the field of providing health services through health maintenance organizations (HMOs).

One afternoon Williams walked into my office and said she had an offer that we could not refuse: "Working for the governor to change Texas!" As I recall, my comments had a bit less enthusiasm, but my curiosity was piqued. A couple of days later Martha and I were escorted into the Governor's Office at the state capitol. The governor was wearing his characteristic blue plaid sports jacket and quickly explained what he wanted. He asked for information about how state employees felt about wages, working conditions, supervision, and opportunities for advancement. He had a businessman's sense that this was part of the equation for getting work done with people and said he wanted the numbers as soon as possible. In less than fifteen minutes we were through, with the understanding that we would create the questionnaire and the governor would see to it that agencies participated and paid for the surveying.

In retrospect, it appears that Governor Clements viewed state government as a business that needed some fixing. Part of the fixing was to see where some problems lay, and you found the problems by asking. Thus, for Clements, being a governor was not presiding or necessarily governing in the sense of regulating. Rather, being a governor was acting to make things operate better, run better. Survey data for the governor was like one set of instruments on the dashboard that told the driver how the car was running.

Clements' view of government as an entity that performs certain tasks and thus can be judged much as a business is—with a concern for what kind of return on investment was being provided—was characteristic of many elected officials by the early 1980s. For the nineteenth and most of the twentieth century elected officials did not typically view government from such a functional or performance perspective. Rather, government was viewed as serving largely a regulatory function, resolving disputes between civil parties, expanding into frontier lands, and administering justice. Only during periods of war mobilization, when large percentages of the population were employed in government activities, did there appear a strong emphasis on goal achievement. Typically, once the victory was achieved, the military forces were shrunk, soldiers demobilized and returned to civilian life, and war materiel either auctioned or placed in storage. However, the growth of government programs during the Franklin D. Roosevelt administration and the continuing war mobilization that became the Cold War during the Truman, Eisenhower, Kennedy, Johnson, Nixon, Ford, Carter, and Reagan administrations created large government enterprises at federal, state, and local levels. In response to the vast sizes of these organizations, federal concerns on budgeting and performance appeared. Such concerns were manifest in the Eisenhower and Kennedy administrations and gave rise to a form of governmental, functional budgeting during the Johnson administration.

Functional budgeting demanded that administrators think through what kinds of outputs were being purchased for a given amount of dollars. A person running a household will think of a budget increase such as a hundred dollars a month as meaning that a few more meals can be taken at restaurants or that a repair on a house or car can be made. A person running a business will think of a budget increase in terms of buying new equipment or hiring new employees to improve or increase production. Functional thinking is directed toward what outcomes are made possible by a specific unit of expenditure. Before the emphasis on functional budgeting in government, increases were made more or less with an eye to the amount of money or the percentage change in the budget. If the Department of the Army received an authorization for a 10 percent increase, then both the Navy and the Air Force argued for equal treatment. The perspective of a functional budget asked the question of how much money was involved in a 10 percent increase and what specific capabilities the increase brought in the ability of a given service to conduct tactical or strategic activities. For example, does a 10 percent increase in the Navy budget mean that the service is able to mount independent navies in both the Pacific and Atlantic?

The major architect of the functional budgeting of the Johnson administration, known as the Planning, Programming, and Budgeting System (PPBS), was Robert McNamara. McNamara was a whiz kid holdover from the Kennedy administration, schooled at MIT, and experienced in developing long-term capital and control budgets for Ford Motors. He applied this experience first to the Defense Department as Johnson's secretary of defense. Impressed with the concept's ability to bring order to large bureaucracies and as a means to arbitrate disputes among the military branches, Johnson extended the use of the concept to all of the federal government.

Thus by the mid-1970s both elected officials and career civil servants began to view government quite differently. Formerly government was seen as simply part of the landscape, a small part of the total economy, and something that gained attention only at election time. Rather than being an entity that could be analyzed, streamlined, and set to tasks with specific timelines, it was an enduring feature of the background of American life. Business, arts, communities, and families were the focal objects in the foreground where attention was devoted.

However, for the Clements generation of elected officials, government was seen via a different metaphor. Rather than government being part of the natural order of things like forests, rivers, and valleys, government was an entity like a machine. Machines are things created by humans and can be designed for different purposes. Moreover, the machine and each of its parts can be examined and judged as to how well it performs its assigned tasks. Thus, asking how employees feel about the performance of their tasks was a natural part of using a machine metaphor to understand and change government.

Development of the Texas Employee Attitude Survey from 1979 to 1992

No research enterprise is independent of either issues of the times or the personal inclinations of the researcher. The original survey design was influenced by climate assessment strategies that I had drawn from early work with community organizations in the 1960s and in the 1970s with Prudential and other companies that sought to improve labor relations and management.

Martha Williams took this framework and gathered additional items from focus groups of state employees and the instrument came to be called the Employee Attitude Survey. Williams had a long-standing interest in promoting opportunities for women, and the instrument included questions about issues pertaining to opportunities for women and minorities. The Employee Attitude Survey was conducted every two years coinciding with the biennial budget of the state. The design of the data collection called for a random draw of approximately 10,000 employees. About a dozen of the largest state agencies were used to create the sample. Large agencies provided an inexpensive strategy for collecting the sample. Data collection was very straightforward. The surveys were duplicated on regular paper, a sample of employees was drawn from each of the chosen twelve or so agencies, and instruments were given to the personnel offices of the agencies to distribute to the employees. Employees returned the surveys in most cases by U.S. mail or by state interagency mail; in some cases, supervisors in the agency collected the completed surveys. The data were then hand-entered by having clerical staff read and record the answers from each instrument. The hand-recorded data were then transferred to computer-readable formats for statistical analyses.

With this data collection and reduction design, the entire process took about twelve months from the distribution of the survey instrument until reports were prepared and returned to the Governor's Office and the participating agencies. The data provided information about how various groupings within the labor force (women, ethnic minorities, various pay classifications, etc.) viewed employment issues. These included perceptions about the quality of supervision, opportunity for advancement, adequacy of equipment, and satisfaction with salary and benefits. Some participating agencies used the data to make changes or provide training on identified topics.

The Texas Employee Attitude Assessment (EAA), as the program came to be called, focused on how the average state employee felt about working for the state. It sought to detect whether particular demographic groups, such as women and minorities, were less well treated than other groups of employees. Variations among state agencies were not fully considered as only about a dozen large agencies provided the sample for the employee pool. In time a variety of item-by-item data analyses were conducted and additional information developed from clusters of questionnaire items using factor analysis to create the following scales in the EAA:

Supervisor Effectiveness—How capable employees feel their supervisor is

Fairness toward Employees—Whether employees feel that appropriate and uniform standards are applied to all

Personnel Office Effectiveness—Whether benefits, salary structure, and training opportunities are clear and meet employees' expectations

Work Group Effectiveness—How effective the employee's immediate working team is perceived to be

Good Job—How appealing the employee finds his or her current job

Time/Stress Management—How well the employee feels he or she can manage time and work demands

Fair Pay/Classification—How fair the employee feels pay is relative to the employee's job classification

Adequacy of the Physical Work Environment—How adequate offices, parking, equipment, and other tools in the work setting are

Affirmative Action—Whether the employee feels that hiring, supervision, and advancement are free from racial, ethnic, and gender bias

As such, the EAA effort remained true to the original concerns of Governor Clements. It sought to detect areas in which individual employee complaints existed and provided leadership information about broadly felt concerns.

The Creation of the Survey of Organizational Excellence

By 1993, the survey goals and procedures were long overdue for a checkup and overhaul. Martha Williams had left the University of Texas, and my academic unit had a new dean, Barbara White. She was eager to expand our activities to improve services in human well-being and to focus energies on crucial issues. At her urging I then picked up the lead responsibility for the existing activity and began a long-term process to create a different instrument and tools to assist organizations in continuous change.

Through the years of EAA and into the creation of the SOE, there were substantial changes in state leadership. Leadership from the Governor's Office had included Mark White, a Democrat, who defeated Clements, and the return of Clements, who defeated Mark White. The White administration began with great promise as the state witnessed the prosperity resulting from the sharp increases in the price of oil that had occurred between 1973 and 1985. Oil had jumped in price from five or six dollars a barrel to over thirty-five dollars in 1985 as the OPEC cartel wrestled control of oil production and pricing from several large international oil companies. While the high price of oil brought pain to most of the country, Texas rolled in riches and Texas government was able to expand without increasing taxes. However, in the fall of 1985 Saudi Arabia cranked up production to discipline oil producers that were exceeding their production quotas. The action caused the price of oil to drop, within weeks, to below ten dollars a barrel. By 1986, Texas was in a depression and the Legislature in revolt.

Business activity had declined and the precipitous drop in oil prices had resulted in an equally sharp decline in tax revenues. The leadership of the state had to both raise taxes and cut spending. To a substantial extent, the defeat of White was due to the crisis in Texas government. Texas could no longer expect to fund government with the painless increase in oil revenues, and oil was rapidly receding as a source of wealth in the state's economy. Many in the state were forced to realize that an economy based upon natural resources—whether raising cattle on the vast prairies, lumbering the great southern forests, or drilling for oil beneath the land—was abruptly winding down! The sudden end to this relatively easy source of wealth would add greater urgency and even some air of crisis to organizations in state government to do business very differently.

Even as political fortunes shifted in the Governor's Office, each office holder recognized the need to continue activities to modernize and improve state government. Ann Richards, a Democrat elected in 1990, continued the support of SOE activity with increased concerns to broaden the characteristics of the membership of the state workforce and improve state government services. Like Clements and White, she was influenced by growing concerns to improve the effectiveness of organizations and placed special importance on increasing quality in state government services. When George Bush defeated Richards, he increased the emphasis of having agencies gather empirical data. He asked that each indicate in agency strategic plans how problems were to be solved and quality promoted. He also emphasized far wider participation by all areas of state government in steps to promote quality and effectiveness.

Governor Bush came to office during a time when Democrats and Republicans often ran against government as a way of becoming the head of the government. Bush did not choose the path of attacking the organizations that he would lead and has continually stressed that government must judiciously choose what its goals are and then accomplish those goals with excellence. Bush has expressed his expectations continually to state employees that he is pleased to lead them and he and they must join in the pursuit of excellence.

Leadership in the Lieutenant Governor's Office, as in the House of Representatives, has seen fewer personalities in this period with William Hobby holding the post in the late 1970s; he was succeeded by Bob Bullock in 1990. Lieutenant Governor Bullock, who had served as the state comptroller during the difficult budget years of the 1980s, was particularly sensitive to the need to control state budgets and get as much return as possible from existing dollars invested in agencies. House leaders Gib Lewis and Pete Laney were equally concerned about costs and quality of state services.

Indeed, the theme to control state budgets led to the collaboration of the Lieutenant Governor's Office, the Speaker of the House's Office, and the State Comptroller's Office under John Sharp to conduct performance reviews of state agencies. These reviews and the creation of the slogan, "Reinventing Government,"[4] generated programs to streamline activity, eliminate redundancy, and generally use a top-down strategy of reorganizing individual governmental units to increase efficiency.

Among leaders from all backgrounds and both major parties was a perception that state government was growing in its responsibilities and that improvement was needed and possible. These concerns have become especially evident in their staff mechanisms, particularly those of the Governor's Office of Budget and Planning and the Legislature's Legislative Budget Office. The devolution of federal funding and direction of health and social programs to the states tremendously increases the size and complexity of activities that states must manage. In Texas the burgeoning population, the changing foundation of the economy, and the demand for higher tax revenues to meet the needs of a growing state place much greater responsibilities on state government. Indeed state government is increasingly viewed by these leaders as an important part of the mix that will help the state develop new jobs and businesses. Moreover, Texas must not only provide more jobs for a growing population but also replace many of the jobs based upon the agricultural and oil foundation that earlier fueled the state's growth and prosperity.

Such leadership concerns have come today to produce a much more demanding atmosphere for governmental heads and their organizations. Rather than accepting assurances from agency leaders that a good job was being done and that a better job would come with more money in the budget, leaders are asking agencies to do more with little or no new funding. Moreover, the questions are of the order of "Have you thought of other ways of doing it?" "What are some more efficient and less costly ways?" "What evidence do you have that you are doing the best possible job?" and so on. Such concerns set the stage for our work to reexamine our survey instrument and procedures and seek ways to improve and streamline these activities.

Texas Leadership's Critique of Past Efforts

The need for a new survey was not just limited to new and increased demands from state and agency leadership for stronger survey data. In the years since the EAA survey had begun, much conceptual and technological advancement had occurred and needed to be incorporated in the instrument. Moreover, many agencies felt that the existing questions needed revisions and that new topics were required. In meetings we held with personnel from the Governor's Office and the Legislative Budget Board, legislators, and state agency officials several specific concerns emerged. The essential ones were as follows:

- The length of time between when data were collected and when reports were delivered was usually about a year. That was too long a time for the data to be used as a description of many conditions since organizations may change substantially in a year.
- More agencies needed to participate. State leaders required information not just about the average state employee, but about how opinions varied from agency to agency. With more than 125 state agencies, exclusive of universities and colleges, information was needed at an agency level.
- More resources were needed in helping agencies use the survey data. Employee data that are collected but seemingly never used by an organization result in the deterioration of employee morale. In addition to data about organizations, clear procedures were needed on how organizations could use such data to improve.

With the growth in the size of the state's population and the greater complexity of the state's business organizations, the need for a broader and more diverse survey was evident. Moreover, the magnification of contacts between state governments and other states and nations, particularly Mexico, which came with economic expansion, placed greater challenges on state government.

To respond to these concerns and to address changes in survey technique and organizational theory, the process for creating a new survey was begun. A detailed protocol was created to guide the development of a new instrument as well as data collection and reporting procedures.

Planning Meetings

Meetings were held with representatives of the Governor's Office and the Lieutenant Governor's Office, staff of the House Appropriations Committee, staff of the Legislative Budget Office, individual

11

legislators, and representatives of individual agencies and agency groups during 1993. From these first meetings we concluded that there was strong interest in continuing the survey, but also that there was substantial need to change the survey instrument, data collection, and reporting methodologies. Two staff members of the Legislative Budget Office, Albert Hawkins and John Barton, led the activities to make certain a tool was created that would pertain to the diversity of state agencies. Both of them worked with us to provide data to assess how well an agency's human resources are used. They helped make certain that the new survey related to the multiple needs of both the executive and legislative side of state leadership. Moreover, they worked hard to convince state agencies that the purpose of collecting such data was not to "micro-manage" organizations, but rather to push all state organizations to become more flexible and innovative.

Focus Groups

Next several focus group sessions were convened in November and December 1993 with agency representatives. At those meetings users identified material that required changing, such as eliminating questions and topics, shortening the amount of time needed to take the survey, and developing procedures to ensure more rapid return of data to the participants. Much of the language of the 1979–1992 survey was viewed as dated, and it was felt that a number of new concepts should be built into the next survey.

After reviewing the commentary from former users of the survey data, we began to assemble new instrument and survey procedures. We focused on creating a survey that could be used by all agencies of Texas government and on keeping costs low so that 100 percent sampling would not be prohibitive.

Pre-Tests

The revised survey was pre-tested in several agencies during the fall of 1993 as length, clarity, and conceptual rigor were refined. As the survey was developed, drafts were provided to users in October, November, and December 1993 who, in turn, provided assessments of the developing instrument. Through the development process, steps were taken to provide some comparability to the past, and specific items in the survey enabled a comparison of attitudes today to those of two years ago. More than twenty pre-tests of the new instrument were taken in state agencies from November 1993 through March 1994. These pre-tests helped to ensure readability, reliability of scales and items, reasonableness in terms of time required to complete the survey, and appropriateness of content and language of every item.

The First Deployment of the Survey of Organizational Excellence

By July 1994, the new survey and procedures were in place. Survey instruments were delivered to fifty-two state agencies where 62,000 surveys were distributed. Surveys were distributed to most agencies through the state mail process from July to October 1994. Completed instruments were returned by the U.S. Postal Service and immediately scanned and accumulated into a database. Data collection was ended in the first week of December, and preliminary results were mailed to all agencies in the third week of December 1994 with final reports provided in March 1995.

Rapid Reporting of Data at Interim Steps

One of the frequent criticisms of the previous instrument was the long wait between the distribution of the instrument to employees and the subsequent presentation of the results to the agency. A second frequent criticism was that the report tended to be a very long document that was tedious to read. Consequently, it served more as a history of employee attitudes than as a tool for making better decisions about needed organizational changes.

Two important steps were taken to address these concerns. One step was to develop a survey that was optically scanned with data reduction procedures that would permit rapid processing of the data. After searching for firms with capability and experience in printing and scanning surveys, J&D Data Services of Plano, Texas, was selected as the contractor to print and scan the instruments. The owner, Joe Deegan, was highly expert in the design and utilization of optically scored instruments and ensured that the new instrument made full use of this technology. Scanned data were stored on computer-readable material, and analyses were conducted almost immediately. This procedure permitted data to be sent to agencies as they became available. This replaced the wait of several months for all information to be presented in a final tabulation. The second step was to make direct data sets available to users rather than voluminous printouts of the data.

The World Wide Web

As an additional aid to rapidly disseminate the information, non-confidential data were loaded on a World Wide Web server, and the

HTTP address was sent to all participating agencies. Narrative descriptions of every participating agency were developed, along with general charts of the survey data, and made available through this Internet service.

The SOE, when distributed to each employer, was accompanied by letters signed by me and from the head of each agency explaining the importance of the survey and assuring that answers would remain confidential and be used to improve organizational functioning. I included my office telephone number in my letter and asked employees to call me if they had any questions about the survey. There were days during the fall that I received as many as forty telephone calls. The content of the calls told us a lot about employee concerns. The most frequent type of call was just to inquire whether I was Mike Lauderdale, the same person who had signed the letter. When I said I was, most of these callers seemed satisfied; some would say they were just checking to make certain that I did exist and the surveys would come to me. The second most frequent call was to ask me how I could assure the caller that his or her identity would be protected. These callers said they had some concerns in their job or in their organization and wanted to let others know of their concern, but they wanted to avoid being the object of retaliation. Almost every caller also wanted to know whether anything would really happen with the results. They would say that surveys had been given before but nothing ever seemed to come of the effort.

Such calls are very telling about issues that must be addressed in any organization. When persons in an organization feel that something is wrong and yet are afraid of being punished or ignored if they speak out, one can safely conclude that supervision or employee selection or some other factor is seriously amiss. For many of these agencies, this was the first time that such a survey had been done. In all cases I emphasized to the callers that the survey was being done at the request of the governor and with the full support of state leadership and the head of each participating agency. In many cases, callers would ask whether this was true. I also emphasized to the callers that each agency had made an independent decision to participate and that not all state agencies had decided to do so. I stressed that any participating agency was dead serious about the importance of the survey and using the results to seek improvements. Callers seemed impressed by the fact that both the top of their organization and the leadership of the state itself wanted this information.

14

Employees returned the SOE in individual envelopes through the U.S. postal system to ensure anonymity. All items on the survey were marked on printed forms and mailed to the contractor. The survey was optically scanned and preliminary data were provided to all agencies by December 1994. The cleaned and refined data set for each agency was distributed in March 1995 to each participating agency and to the Governor's Office. Narrative descriptions of agencies and nonconfidential SOE data were posted on the Web server by May 1995. Thus, the twelve months or so from survey distribution to return of results required by the EAA were cut to no more than seven months.

Advances in the 1996–1997 SOE

Advancements were continued in the 1996–1997 SOE, further reducing the length of time between survey administration and return of the data. Surveys were distributed in July, August, September, and October. Each agency received its data by the end of October, and statewide results were released in December. No agency waited more than three months before its data were returned, and many received data within thirty days after surveys were distributed to personnel! Such rapid return of the data increased the likelihood that the data got to leadership quickly enough to provide an accurate and contemporary description of the organization. One of the more striking aspects of the 1996–1997 SOE was the response rate. In the 1994–1995 survey, the statewide agency response rate was 32 percent. In 1996–1997 the rate increased to 52 percent. Clearly, state employees were viewing the SOE as part of a genuine compact between state and agency leadership and all employees to identify areas of excellence and quickly discover areas needing attention.

During this time period average employee turnover was a bit over 10 percent per year. This could produce some inherent skew in the data in that the most dissatisfied employees could regularly disappear between administrations of the SOE by leaving the organization. Conversations with personnel officers in many of the organizations suggest that employees have a variety of reasons for ending employment: changing circumstances (spouses finding employment in another city), better job offers, changing family relationships, career changes, and so on. Large-scale employee turnover will indeed affect the comparisons of SOE scores between administrations, and this is evident in smaller organizations.

Benchmarking against Best Practices

Other improvements were added to the 1996–1997 SOE. A formal, external benchmarking group was created to advise on how such surveys are used in large and competitive private business organizations. Outstanding private businesses were selected that were well known for the soundness of their organization and their capabilities in developing human resources within the organization.[5] This group has become the SOE *benchmark for best practices.* This group, along with representatives from many of the agencies, participated in a startup meeting just before the distribution of the SOE in July 1996. The committee, termed the Corporate Benchmarking Committee, shared their experience of the competitive necessity of having such survey data and how their corporations used the data to improve quality and competitiveness. The membership of the benchmarking committee includes representatives from large, international high-technology companies and from the hotly competitive and rapidly changing health service field. Current membership of the committee is shown in the list below.

Mr. Tommy Schmitt, Director, Employee Assistance Program (K14), Motorola

Mr. Leo Dunn, Staff Vice President for Corporate Services, 3M Corporation, Austin

Dr. Norman Chenven, Chief Executive Officer, Austin Regional Clinic

Mr. Keith Brewer, Program Manager for Re-Engineering Operations, IBM Server Group, IBM

Mr. Woody Gilliland, Chief Executive Officer, Abilene Regional Medical Center

Michael Kelly, Ph.D., Professor, University of Missouri at Columbia

Summary

To date the Survey of Organizational Excellence has been used by over seventy-five different public and private organizations with more than 200,000 instruments distributed. In addition to Texas, the use of the SOE is now underway in several other states, including Missouri, Florida, and Arizona, and with other levels of government and private business. It is included in the directives for establishing the formal strategic plan for all state agencies in Texas as required by the Governor's Office and the Legislative Budget Board.[6] Data benchmarks are now available for many types of organizations, organizational levels, and demographic characteristics and include data such as that shown below.

Size:
　Under 50 employees
　50–99 employees
　100–999 employees
　1,000–50,000 employees
Gender:
　Male
　Female
Ethnicity:
　African-American
　Anglo-American
　Hispanic-American
Pay levels:
　Under $10,000
　$10,000–14,999
　$15,000–19,999
　$20,000–24,999
　$25,000–29,999
　$30,000–34,999
Agency mission:
　Regulatory
　Law enforcement
　Health
　Human services
　Manufacturing

In eighteen years the SOE has evolved from a concern about employee attitudes expressed by a governor to a tool endorsed by four governors from both major political parties and the leadership of the Texas Legislature. A continuously improving tool, it is used to quantify human resources in organizations and assist in establishing goals for improvement. It is available as an optically scanned instrument as well as through the Internet as a secure HTML version. Benchmarking data and practices among agencies are available as well as comparison information with a cohort of highly advanced high-technology and health care businesses.

The SOE data and related participation patterns have begun an important chain of events in building a general atmosphere of heightened importance of organizational performance in state government. Dozens of specific applications of agencies using the data to pinpoint problems, involve employees, and improve processes have been established. Chapter 6 provides many such examples, and the SOE Web site continues to chronicle this change process.

2 | The Survey Concept in Organizational Development

In an era of decreasing budgets, rapid change, and astonishing environmental complexity, organizations must have an organizational culture that develops and supports employees who are committed, innovative, efficient, and characterized by diversity. Data-based internal assessments provide an important dimension by which to assess organizational strengths and weaknesses, the effects of leadership changes, and progress over time. Clearly, the most readily available asset for improving organizational performance is a better understanding of the organization's human resources, its people.

The following observations, ideas, and procedures detail how the best organizational procedures should be implemented to provide data for organizational improvement. They represent the approach used in the implementation of the Survey of Organizational Excellence.

Methods for Collecting Internal Data

Finding out what employees think about their workplace is inherently difficult. Some employees fear the loss of opportunities, income, or even their jobs if their employer finds out the true nature of their feelings. While others may be eager to share their views and ideas for change, opportunities for them to do so are often limited or ineffective. Even after internal data (employee perceptions) are collected, the information may raise more questions in the organization than it provides answers. When interpreting internal data, common questions may include the following: how broadly is a given concern held among employees? do concerns exist among employees that are not reported in the data? how stable are the concerns over time?

A variety of tools and procedures are available for acquiring employee perceptions. These include the employee suggestion box, focus groups, agency retreats with discussion groups, employee bulletin boards (electronic and traditional), telephone polls, observations of supervisors, occasional comments from employees and employee representatives (e.g., unions, professional and trade associations), and the like. While each of these tools is useful, research and practice have shown that the successful application of each tool requires considerable thought. Each method will result in information that is greatly influenced by the manner in which the data are collected and to whom the data are given.

Each of these methods can offer an organization important information about what employees think. However, standardized formal surveys are the most representative and practical option for assessing the overall organizational culture. Such surveys are the superior tool for quantifying these concerns because they allow input from everyone in the organization, protect employee anonymity, encourage thoughtful, careful responses, and facilitate the transition of information to quantifiable, measurable organizational goals. Surveys are the most effective when participation is maximized. The goal should be for all employees to be given a survey and be encouraged to respond.

Optimally, once problematic issues are identified, the organization should follow up the written survey with other, less extensive internal data collection methods, such as focus groups and observations of employee interactions. These steps are taken to identify *why* employees responded as they did on the survey and to determine what changes should be implemented to alleviate problem areas. When written surveys are followed by strategically targeted data collection activities, they result in a very thorough, effective tool for improvement. Used in this combination, the organization will gain a comprehensive view of the strengths and weaknesses that exist and, more importantly, will have determined what must be accomplished to move the organization closer to achieving its mission.

Reasons for Conducting Employee Surveys

Reliable and effective means of communication between management and employees are necessary for productive, successful workplaces. The most critical challenge for most organizations is how to get information from frontline workers to top leadership. In most organizations, top-down communication from the chief executive officer to the frontline employee involves a systematic, defined process that enables organizational leaders to communicate the vision, procedures, and goals of the organization to all. In contrast, communication from the bottom up is often fraught with difficulties and obstacles, such as supervisory restrictions, physical distance, and the lack of opportunity. Employee attitude surveys supplement traditional means of communication and ensure the flow of communication from the bottom up.

Check the Pulse of the Organization

Employee attitude surveys originated in large organizational settings. They were used for various reasons but mainly as a response to labor-management conflicts and attempts at employee unionization. The early surveys were used to check the pulse of the workforce, in particular to determine employees' level of satisfaction with pay and benefits and whether the organization was vulnerable to unionization.

Unions in America have played important roles in creating improved salaries, working conditions, and benefits for workers. They have been instrumental in promoting literacy, citizenship, and civic responsibility for immigrants. Nevertheless, they developed in response to inadequate or, worse, exploitative leadership in organizations. Thus, unionization is an important predictor of leadership failure in an organization. Unions rise, typically, because of conflict between employees and leadership.[1]

This organizational status check remains a common reason for conducting employee surveys. Just as physicians conduct routine physical examinations to check the health and functioning of their patients, an employee survey similarly checks the health of an organization.

An adequate physical examination provides one of two answers. One answer is that the person is in good health. He or she should be encouraged to continue the actions that help maintain healthy status—such as eating right, exercising regularly, getting enough sleep, and others. The other answer is that some particular body function or health measure is operating out of the bounds of healthy functioning.

Perhaps breathing is labored, blood chemistry indicates an elevation of low-density cholesterol, or blood pressure is somewhat high. When the general physical provides some information that a specific indicator is giving out-of-range readings, then additional tests are used to pinpoint with greater exactness the problem. A regularly given physical examination also permits an overtime comparison of the health status of the individual. The physician and the patient can then use both the general benchmarks of what a comparable person's health indicators are and the historical pattern of the individual patient.

A similar logic should be used with organizational surveys. The SOE as described here is analogous to a physical examination for the organization. It reports several broad and essential measures of the organization. Reference benchmarks are available both to comparable organizations and to previous scores using the instrument. Like the general physical for individuals, the tool helps to identify problems early and to direct interventions logically to areas of concern or weakness. This is a particularly important advantage given both the size of the investment the organization is making in human resources and the need to continually improve the capabilities of employees.

Sometimes, however, the inventory of training, consultation, and organizational development resources that an organization is using looks a lot like a hypochondriac's medicine cabinet. Every popular cure in the media and from the professions is being used, and in some cases the organizational interventions, like drugs in the medicine cabinet, are antagonistic. If the organization is lucky, just resources are being wasted.

The SOE is an alternative to these shots in the dark. The idea behind a regular general survey is to create a baseline measure and then proceed in an informed and professional manner to select tools for further definition of problems. This permits problems to be addressed in a proper order and interventions to be selected that logically relate to a total perspective on the organization.

Measure Progress toward Goals

Employee surveys provide a quantifiable assessment of employees' perceptions of the organization's progress toward established goals. They assist organizations to determine the effects of various initiatives and to measure critical workplace characteristics such as quality concerns, empowerment, job satisfaction, stress management, and burnout. The information provided by the SOE enables an organization to compare information across organizational divisions or other group-ings at a specific point in time and over the life of the organization.

Hear from Everyone in the Organization

True to the saying "The squeaky wheel gets the grease," managers of-ten find themselves hearing from and responding to the same people repeatedly. This is a variant of Pareto's observation that less than 20 percent of events require a disproportionate amount of organiza-tional attention.[2] These employees, the "squeaky wheels," frequently become a black hole, absorbing most of managers' time and attention. On the other hand, some employees feel uncomfortable talking about their concerns with their supervisors. This reluctance may have a va-riety of causes, including fear of retaliation or not wanting to be seen as "complaining." Thus, the "squeaky wheels" drive a perception of the organization that may be highly distorted. By using anonymous surveys, managers can hear from individuals in the organization who may be less apt to voice concerns. In addition, survey data can provide managers at the highest levels of the organization with information that comes directly from employees without being altered by others in the organization's chain of command.

Send a Positive Message to Employees

The act of administering an employee survey, in itself, can contribute to a more positive work environment. It sends a message that man-agement is concerned and interested in what employees think, that employees are a valued organizational resource and that management is committed to improving the workplace. The regular use of a survey signals that the organization's culture seeks information and engages in continuous improvement.

Schedule

Employee surveys are the most beneficial to organizations when con-ducted on a regular basis. When routinely scheduled, the information becomes a valuable record of organizational progress and a reliable tool to guide management decisions, as opposed to a haphazard event that may have limited impact on the organization.

A routine, regular survey schedule helps to counter one of the most commonly voiced reasons for not conducting an employee survey: "Our organization is going through so many changes that it's not a good time." However, organizational change events, such as a leadership change, a crisis, or a reorganization or downsizing, should serve as a signal that an employee survey is needed. Surveys provide benchmark measures to evaluate the impact of organizational change over time. Surveys help to determine the effectiveness of organizational changes and provide clues as to any unidentified or hidden costs associated with organizational events, such as loss of employee morale, increased stress, and communication problems.

In a time of tight budgets yet increasing demands, there will never be a "perfect" time to conduct an employee survey. Change is the status quo. However, a regular survey schedule gives the organization a constant reference point by which to measure the effects of change on *internal* aspects of the organization, which ultimately determine how well *external* customers are served.

Many organizations conduct employee surveys annually; however, a schedule should be determined based on the unique needs of the organization, available resources, and the degree of changes occurring in the organization's environment. Organizations with relatively stable internal and external environments may find annual or biennial surveys satisfactory. In contrast, an organization with a constantly changing environment may need more current information to be able to meet new demands. The most important point is that organizations must regularly and uniformly collect objective information on employee attitudes. Avoiding that responsibility is similar to a business that never balances its books or a person who puts off physical exams. Such neglect of fundamental actions is a prescription for serious organizational problems.

Survey Participation and the One Hundred Percent Solution

With resources constrained in most organizations due to increased competition in private markets and for revenues in the public sector, all organizations are faced with doing "more with less." What is becoming increasingly evident in this environment is that every organizational member must be ready to learn new tasks and to take on new responsibilities. Every position is critical to organizational success. Employees in all positions must contribute fully to the organization to achieve its mission. Consequently, employee surveys should include participation for the total organization—*the One Hundred Percent Solution.* Striving to get a participation rate of 100 percent rather than a sample yields an important advantage. A 100 percent sample does not serve to promote alienation that invariably occurs through sampling. While a much smaller sample can often provide suitable accuracy to forecast general population characteristics, it has unintended negative side effects for an organization. It gives the impression that people are inanimate objects like widgets on an assembly line. Grab two or three, measure, average the scores, and you have a pretty good estimate of the total population. Sampling is economical and statistically appropriate, but it betrays a complete misunderstanding of why you do an organizational survey. Part of the inherent methodology of an organizational survey should be to get everyone on board.

When all organizational members are invited to provide input via the survey, the organization benefits in many ways:
• The entire survey process is viewed more positively by both employees and management.
• Managers are less apt to think that only the most disgruntled employees responded to the survey; they are therefore more inclined to act on survey results.
• When management communicates to employees that everyone is being asked to participate in the survey, employees get a sense that the individual is valued by the organization.
• Complete participation engenders greater trust in the survey process because employees will not fear that they have been somehow singled out by management and that the results may be used against them.

The Survey Process

The survey process is best viewed as an ongoing, cyclic activity that leads the organization through the activities necessary to reach the desired, improved state. The cycle of the survey process has several phases, including goal setting, administration, feedback-critique, and ownership-action and refocusing.

Phase 1: Goal Setting

The first phase involves setting organizational goals for the survey and establishing a structure by which to achieve the goals. One of the most important questions that leadership should ask before initiating a survey is "What do we want to accomplish?" The answers to this question should be formulated into goals that steer the vision of the survey process. Goals may be as straightforward as simply assessing general morale or as complex as benchmarking to previous change efforts. Based on the size of the organization, goals may be established at many different levels, such as organization-wide, regional, divisional, programmatic, or local.

For instance, in an organization that has recently implemented a flexible working hours policy, one of the goals of the survey may be to establish how this new policy is affecting employees' job satisfaction and time and stress management. Survey results addressing these areas may be compared to previous surveys to determine if there has been a change in perceptions that could possibly be attributed to the new policy. On a smaller scale, the technical assistance department of the management information systems division may establish goals to measure the satisfaction of their customers—the employees of the organization. Appropriately, designed surveys should permit one to see organization-wide characteristics and properties of all smaller sub-units as well. An important aspect of an organizational survey can be to determine how well needs of internal customers are being met.

Develop a Plan of Action

A well-designed plan of action will assist the organization to achieve its survey goals. The primary purpose of the plan should be to develop a structure by which members of the organization can communicate survey findings and facilitate organizational improvements.

At a minimum, a plan of action should include the following:

1. *Who will coordinate the survey process.* "Survey Coordinators" and "Survey Steering Committees" are frequently used in organizations conducting employee attitude surveys. These persons coordinate and guide the activity for the entire organization, frequently including activities such as directing survey administration and analyzing and reporting "big picture" survey results to the executive staff and employees. Who is appointed to coordinate the survey should be based on how the organization intends to use survey results. Steering committees consisting of individuals from throughout the organization are particularly effective if the membership is made up of a "diagonal slice" down and across the organization. This diagonal slice includes persons from various departments and staff levels. Such membership brings expertise, perspective, and experience from across the organization.

2. *How results will be used to achieve the organization's goals.* Organizations may want to use quality improvement structures, such as employee quality teams or circles, which already exist within the organization to facilitate improvement. In other situations, a new committee may be expected to further progress toward the goals. How-

ever, in almost all situations, existing organizational structures—divisions, managers, and teams—should share the responsibility of using the results to reach the goals.

3. *A timeline for achieving goals.* The plan should be in place before the release of survey results. The survey is a tool to provide internal data about employee perceptions. Effective leadership will use the data as part of a plan for organizational improvement. A plan should proceed the survey so that when the results are available, the information gets to managers and employees in a timely manner. Without a plan in place, the organization runs the risk that the survey process will not be effective. The results may come back to the organization and be perceived unfavorably, and then little is done with them. A plan should drive the organization closer to its improvement goals and keep the process on schedule.

Communicate with Employees

The implementation of a survey is an excellent opportunity for leadership to call for the highest efforts of employee commitment and excellence. Thus, it is mandatory for top leadership to communicate with employees about the survey prior to its administration. The upcoming survey should be announced, the goals for the process should be introduced, participation should be encouraged, and employees should be told what they can expect to happen when survey results are finalized. Several other communication issues should be dealt with at this time, including respondent anonymity, the importance of employee participation, and organizational plans for follow up.

Anonymity

Trust and assurances of confidentiality are relevant concerns for employees in any organization. Management can help reassure employees about the confidentiality of the survey process by dealing with the issue in the open. The more that management can do to reassure employees that there will be no attempt to find the identity of respondents, the more comfortable employees will feel with the survey process. This will increase the likelihood that employees will respond to the survey in the most complete, candid, and thoughtful manner.

Response Rate

The response rate is the number of respondents divided by the total number of surveys distributed. The response rate that yields a valid and representative sample in a mail-out survey is partially a function of the size of the organization and the degree to which the demographic characteristics of the sample parallel those dimensions in the organization. However, it is safe to conclude that the higher the response rate, the more the data are a valid representation of the opinions of the workforce.

The survey response rate is a critical issue for several reasons. The number of employees that respond to a survey will affect whether survey findings are seen as a reliable tool for organizational improvement activities. However, a low response rate can also be a diagnostic measure in itself for the organization. The lack of employee participation in surveys may suggest several issues, such as low morale, heavy work load and burn-out, too many or too frequent surveys, or lack of management follow-up on previous surveys. In addition, low levels of employee participation in the survey can defeat one of the most valuable aspects of employee surveys, that of promoting the idea that organizational improvement is a shared responsibility between leadership and employees. Clearly, when outside groups view response-rate data, high rates are seen as more favorable.

With some advanced planning, organizations can increase the level of employee participation to ensure reliable data and to achieve other organizational benefits. The following tips gleaned from our experiences help to secure maximum participation:

1. Build anticipation among employees about the survey. Communicating to employees when the survey will take place, what the organization's goals for the survey are, and how the results will be used generates anticipation. Some of the best methods by which to communicate these messages can include employee newsletters, e-mail messages, memos from the head of the agency, bulletin boards, and staff meetings.

2. Announce that survey results will be shared with employees and included in the organization's strategic plan. If employees know that they and others will see the results of the survey, they are more likely to respond. Individuals involved in coordinating the survey should determine in advance what results will be released to employees and when and how it will be accomplished. These decisions are customarily based on the goals of the survey and the size of the organization.

3. Emphasize that respondents' anonymity will be maintained. Previous survey experiences reveal that, in almost all organizations, trust is a significant issue for employees. Many employees express great concern that their employer may be able to trace responses back to

them. Information that the organization distributes about the survey should include reminders that assurances are in place to prevent the employing organization from identifying respondents.

4. Get individuals from throughout the organization involved in the survey process. The more individuals perceive that they have a "hand" in the survey process, the more likely they are to respond. For instance, developing customized questions serves as a good opportunity to include others. In addition, leaders of employee groups, such as a cultural committee and other specialized employee interest groups, should be included in survey discussions so that they can provide input and return the information to the employee group.

5. Follow up the survey distribution with a reminder to employees. Approximately ten days after surveys are distributed, the organization should send out a reminder asking employees to respond and return the survey if they have not already done so. This message should include the date when data collection will be closed for the organization (typically, we close data collection six weeks after distribution).

6. Follow up on the survey findings. The response to future surveys is highly dependent upon whether employees perceive that their input has resulted in organizational changes. Improvements that result from survey findings should be communicated to employees.

Follow-up Plans

The most helpful activity for increasing employee response to the survey is to communicate how the organization will follow up on survey findings. Employees want to know that their input will be heard. If management communicates its plans to follow up on survey findings, employees are more likely to take the time to fill out and return the survey. Employees do not expect that the organization can address every problem highlighted in the survey, but they do want to know that management has a plan to follow up on at least some of the problems.

Agency Examples

The following examples summarize how some Texas state agencies prepared for the 1996–1997 SOE.

Adam Jones, survey liaison for the Texas Education Agency (TEA), conducted a media campaign to enhance awareness of the SOE among TEA employees. The campaign's theme was "Put your two cents in" and included posters that were designed with a picture of two pennies. The primary message of the campaign was that employees' input was important and a valuable part of improving services for the agency's customers, both internal and external. These announcements were posted throughout the building—in elevators, on bulletin boards, and in the cafeteria.

The Texas Department of Housing and Community Affairs (TDHCA) put information about the SOE on a flyer included in employees' paychecks. Cynthia Wells, survey liaison for TDHCA, suggests this method as a good way to get employees' attention and to encourage their participation.

Brian Francis, survey liaison for the Texas Real Estate Commission (TREC), says that his agency uses "town hall" meetings as one avenue to encourage employees to respond to the SOE. These meetings also provide an opportunity to communicate about 1994–1995 SOE results. Brian believes that the "town hall" meetings are very effective. With so many members of the workforce present (as many as seventy-two of the agency's eighty-six employees have attended at one time), the agency-wide meetings ensure that employees hear the same information about a variety of topics that affect the organization. Brian related that one of the benefits of the meetings has been communicating to employees that the SOE is one way by which employees can communicate their thoughts about the organization to management. He says that TREC's leadership stresses that the data belong to the employees, not management, and this message has resulted in a sense of shared responsibility for the state of the organization.

Ann Cook and Morris Winn, survey liaisons for the Texas Department of Insurance (TDI), report that TDI did something new this year to encourage SOE participation. TDI provided a "Survey Room" for employees designed to "separate" employees from office distractions in order to maximize the survey response rate. In the event that the employee wants to mail the survey form on the spot, he or she can place their sealed envelope in a mail container in the room. Anonymity of survey results is maintained in this setting. Information about the Survey Room is distributed to employees through channels such as intra-agency e-mail and bulletin board postings.

The Texas Youth Commission (TYC) uses "video newsletters" to communicate with employees. These videos are produced on a monthly basis by the executive director, and they include information about TYC as well as answers to questions submitted by employees. The videos are disseminated to field locations and are a required part of staff meetings. Eric Young, TYC survey liaison, says that the newsletters are used to encourage employees to participate in the SOE.

According to Chris Cook and JoAnne McElyea, survey liaisons for the Texas Department of Protective and Regulatory Services (TDPRS), TDPRS held a campaign to encourage employee participation in the SOE by including information about the survey in the employee newsletter. The following excerpt is from an article that appeared in an employee newsletter:

Have you been dying to tell someone what you think about the agency's effectiveness, how well you are adapting to new challenges, budget decreases and workload increases, the effectiveness of training, or your state employment benefits?

Are you in luck! Within the next two months, you'll be receiving a copy of the "Survey of Organizational Excellence," and you can give your opinions on these and lots of other topics.

The Survey was originally begun in 1979 to determine if state government meets the needs of a growing and changing state and has been continued by The University of Texas School of Social Work to measure quality over time and among agencies. Your answers will help provide a profile of our agency's strengths and weaknesses so we can celebrate, as well as make improvements where they're needed.

So, put in your 2-cents worth when the Survey arrives. Your opinion can make a difference.

Phase 2: Administration

The administration phase of the survey includes all of the steps necessary for the distribution of the survey forms to employees and their return. When the survey is conducted by an outside entity, the organization usually has few responsibilities during this phase. In these situations, the most helpful activity that the organization can do is to encourage employees to respond to the survey.

There are many advantages in having an outside entity conduct the survey administration. Employees are more likely to respond honestly because they have less fear of their identity being revealed. Moreover, the results of a survey administered by an outsider are usually viewed more objectively by all in the organization because no one can "put a spin" on the results. In addition, it is more cost-effective for the organization to contract for the survey with an outside entity than to develop the knowledge and resources internally.

We use the following procedures for survey distribution.

• The SOE administration phase begins once survey packets are shipped to the organization's survey liaison. Our Survey Office will notify the liaison as to when to expect the box(es). Upon arrival, the survey liaison sees that the survey packets are distributed via intra-agency mail. Once the surveys have been distributed, the liaison notifies the survey coordinator in our office. Data collection for most organizations will be closed six weeks from the date of survey distribution.

· Each survey packet received by employees participating in the SOE includes a cover letter from the organization's executive director/commissioner, the survey instrument, an organization-specific insert, and a self-addressed, stamped envelope.

· Each return envelope is stamped with a multi-digit number. This number (the organization code) will be used to identify surveys coming from employees in each specific organization but do not permit the individual to be identified. The purpose of this number is explained to employees in the cover letter.

Phase 3: Feedback-Critique

This phase of the process begins when the survey results are returned to the organization. It is guided by the plan of action designed during Phase 1. This plan will vary greatly across organizations due to the tremendous differences in the size of organizations and location(s) of the employees participating in the survey.

There is no single best way to analyze and report back data; however, there are best practices in using survey data. *Best practices urge that the data be returned to all members of the organization in a fashion to maximize examination and thoughtful interpretation.*

This is a very important juncture in the survey process. In organizations where conflict has long been suppressed, there may be an atmosphere when results are released of "I told you so" or "Okay, now the cat is out of the bag." What is critically important at this moment is not to head the organization down the road of assigning blame. In setting the tone of the critique process, the organization's leadership should attempt to figure out why there is a problem and what the answer is. Central to the effectiveness of Phase 3 is to build some positive anticipation of finding some flaws, some areas of weaknesses. No organization can ever be perfect. "Critique" means that it is understood that there are problems and the purpose of this phase is to discover where improvements can be made!

Analyzing survey data, reporting results to members of the organization, and obtaining feedback from the organization's members are activities that should result in specific improvement plans. These tasks are best viewed as concurrent processes that feed upon each other. Data are analyzed and reported to the organization, whose members generate responses (qualitative data) that affect data interpretation, which, in turn, generates other questions. If analyses and data reporting do not accompany opportunities for comments, the organization misses opportunities to find out why problems exist. Feedback is necessary to help explain survey data and to move the organization to the next phase, the implementation of specific improvement plans. Common methods to acquire these qualitative data include employee focus groups or staff meetings.

Why Organizations Should Release Survey Results to Employees

Critical to this phase is establishing opportunities to communicate survey findings to employees. This process should be viewed as the fundamental foundation for all improvement activities that follow. *The very act of returning survey results to employees is a powerful organizational intervention.* It says that we are all in this effort together. Simply returning the data enhances trust, openness, and communication.

Survey results should be released to employees to prevent unwarranted damage to morale and trust. When employees respond to a survey, they know only what they think about the workplace. They are usually unaware if others in the organization share similar perceptions. If results are not returned, employees will conclude the worst. The survey results begin to be thought of as a bad report card that must be swept under the rug or hidden in a lower desk drawer by those in charge. By releasing survey results, employees are able to see how their perceptions match with others in the workforce. They are able to identify both the strengths and the weaknesses that exist in the organization rather than concluding that the report contained no good news.

Perhaps the most important reason for returning survey results to employees is to facilitate a sense of shared ownership for the current state of the organization; it increases employees' sense of accountability for the work performed by the organization. Traditionally, surveys have been presented to employees differently. Employees did their part by filling out the survey and then they waited for management to respond. However, lasting and significant change cannot take place without involvement from all in the organization. The survey strategy part of a broader and newer paradigm includes partnering with employees and openly discussing issues raised by the survey.

How to Release Survey Results

Some of the most common settings for presenting survey results to employees include organization meetings, departmental staff meetings, and employee training programs. Many organizations use a combination of these settings as well as written reports via employee newsletters or electronic mail to release survey results to members of the organization. Actual examples and graphic displays (bar graphs, pie charts) facilitate employee understanding. In addition, it is helpful to release data gradually to build interest and prevent persons from being overwhelmed by all of the information.

What Survey Results Should Be Released

Organizational leaders frequently have concerns about how much information should be returned to employees. There are several correct answers to this question. Some organizations release all survey results to employees, while others provide employees with only the "big picture." It is likely that the amount of data returned to employees is less important than one would think; it is the *act* of releasing the results that is the most critical step. Due to traditional survey practices where employees were rarely informed of results, many employees are often skeptical about ever having the opportunity to see survey results. Once the organization begins to release results, the skepticism fades, and the quantity of data actually returned becomes less important to employees. They become more interested in the improvement actions that result from the survey than in every detail contained in the survey report.

How much data will be released to employees is a decision that should be made based on the goals of the survey and discussed before survey results become available to the organization. The important point is that the release of data should be tied to actions to improve specific aspects of the organization.

Phase 4: Ownership-Action and Refocusing

This phase involves the implementation of solutions to address problem areas identified during the feedback-critique activities of Phase 3. It is important to set a cultural condition for the organization that the problems identified are "owned by everyone." While a specific action may fall to one person or one unit of the organization, the ownership of the problem and the solution must be everyone's responsibility. No single person or organizational unit can be permitted to take the stance of "Well, we've got our stuff right; now others must straighten out their mess!" Effective ownership-action means that everyone sees the mission of the total organization and gets the concept of the chain being no stronger than its weakest link.

Organizations should appoint specific persons accountable for improvement activities, and the organization should have plans to evaluate the effectiveness of these changes. All improvement activities taking place in the organization should be communicated to employees and linked back to survey results. Review sessions must be scheduled to examine progress made toward goals and to determine what must be done to refocus the organization to maintain its mission.

A Word of Caution: Survey Hazards

Employee surveys can be a powerful tool for improving the organization; however, surveys that are not conducted properly can do more harm than good. Some of the most common problems associated with employee surveys are the following:

1. *Failing to address employee expectations of improvement.* This is likely to be the most damaging misuse of employee surveys. Employee surveys inherently raise employees' expectations by implying that some form of action will follow the administration of a survey. If employees do not hear anything from management after the survey has ended, they can become suspicious and disillusioned. Fewer employees will respond to surveys in the future and employee cynicism and alienation are increased. Whatever the results of the survey, employers must provide subsequent information to the employees. Emphatically, changes that result from employee surveys should be communicated to employees, linking them back to opinions expressed in the survey.

2. *Failing to ask "why."* When survey results highlight areas of concern, it is important to understand why employees perceive that a particular issue is problematic. This implies open discussion with employees about areas that the survey establishes as weaknesses, creating a sense of shared ownership for the problems, and involving employees in finding solutions. Often problems detected in the survey may simply be the result of misperceptions and can be resolved by involving employees in this communication process.

3. *Failing to view survey results as a tool.* The principal value of a survey is not found in the survey results report; it is found in the discussion and action that ensue after organizational problems are identified. Unfortunately, due to the quantitative nature of the survey results, it is easy to view this information as a definitive report on managers' abilities. The best way to prevent this survey hazard is for upper management to continuously communicate that the survey is a tool for improvement. Attention should be focused on follow-up actions that occur as a result of survey findings. This is a very important

organizational cultural dimension. Organizations that continuously achieve excellence are organizations that actively search for problems to solve. Survey data must be seen as establishing opportunities for improvement.

4. *Failing to address the "whole organization."* Survey data are customarily available at many different levels of analysis. A common data breakout includes organizational divisions or departments. These data breakouts provide information on whether perceptions are universally held throughout the organization or differ due to the environment of particular work areas or other issues. While it is helpful to gain the perspective of various internal differences, an organization may promote comparisons at the expense of understanding the issues affecting the whole organization. Often it is important as well to look at why there may be differences among internal units (i.e., lack of resources, new technology). An important challenge facing most organizations is keeping people aware that achieving quality and excellence is everyone's business. Shortcomings in a single area of the organization ultimately detract from the whole organization.

Moving toward the Self-Reflective Organization

The use of organizational surveys is a crucial part of the process of developing *self-reflective* organizations. Such organizations are, indeed, *thinking* or *learning* organizations. These organizations think about vision, goals, and progress—how well the organization as a total entity is succeeding in reaching goals. Employee attitudes such as "Ours is not to reason why" or "I'm not responsible for things, I just work here" must simply be banished. Employees and the total organization must know the vision, the purpose, and the goals of the organization. They must know, as well, how each task relates to the vision of the organization. For the organization to become self-reflective, data must be gathered regularly about internal functioning and made available to all organization participants. These data then become the *common ground* upon which organizational improvements can be based.

Aligning Organizations

Modern organizations must be conceived as highly complex entities that have hundreds of internal processes and interact with the environment of clients, customers, and suppliers in dozens of ways. One of the major challenges for all such organizations is to keep the organization *aligned* toward its goals, and all processes themselves appropriately aligned to support the organization. An organization is like an exceedingly complex airplane. An airplane has dozens of instruments that report data on processes that serve to keep the airplane properly aligned on its flight path. An altimeter reports how high the airplane is above the ground. An airspeed indicator reports the plane's rate of movement through the air. Compasses and gyroscopes report the direction of flight. Sensors provide engine information on temperature and rate of fuel consumption. Radios, radar, and telemetry devices help to place the plane relative to the earth, other planes, and weather formations. Indeed, a modern airplane is as much a complex information system as anything else, and the information is central to keeping the plane aligned to its goal. The same concept of information to maintain alignment is a crucial concept for modern organizations. Surveys are a critical aspect of internal information that helps keep all employees aligned toward organizational goals.

Inherent Theoretical Model

The theoretical organizational model inherent in using the SOE processes as described in this book is an organization that seeks to fully mobilize the resources of all employees. Moreover, it is an organization that continually yet purposively changes to meet opportunities and challenges and improves products and services—in other words, a *self-reflective* organization, a thinking or learning organization (see figure). To create this sort of organization, data must be acquired on

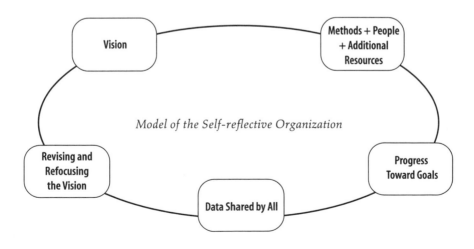

Model of the Self-reflective Organization

37

many dimensions, both external and internal. The SOE data are one crucial element of the internal data.

Summary

This chapter has examined how surveys have come to be used in organizational development. It includes a number of best-practice procedures on how to design and use an organizational survey. The next chapter focuses on how the SOE is constructed and how the data are used.

3 | Guidelines for Understanding the SOE Data

Introduction to Survey Data

Employee attitude surveys generate data that are designed to provide information about the organization's culture and other important attributes of its workforce. Organizations that participate in the Survey of Organizational Excellence receive information about not only employee perceptions but also facts about how perceptions vary among the various groups in an organization. This information includes:

· How those perceptions may change over time
· How they may vary by individual work environments
· How they may be influenced by a variety of demographic characteristics such as gender, ethnicity, and income or pay level

For larger organizations, regional geographical or community variables may also be compared. With all of these complex data available, it can be a daunting task to determine not only where to begin but how to use survey data to generate solutions and organizational improvements.

The next few pages examine the structure of the SOE instrument. This information will assist organizations in understanding and interpreting SOE data, whether the aim is to develop a detailed data-based analysis of the organization or to simply to gain a "big picture" perspective of the issues.

Using Benchmarks

Any property or characteristic has relevance only in comparison to something else. For example, a person is tall or short only when compared with other persons. A fourth-grader who is five feet in height is tall compared with other fourth-graders but short compared with high-schoolers. An automobile is a fast mode of transportation compared with a horse but slow compared with an airplane. To assess the quality of an organization's products or services requires finding some comparable products or services from another organization.

One of the important strengths of the SOE is that many of the questions and general descriptions of organizational conditions that are made available through the instrument permit direct comparisons with other organizations. This is an invaluable attribute of the SOE since it permits leadership to benchmark qualities of their organizations against other organizations. Such comparisons are a very important part of creating competitive standards for an organization and breaking out of the "business as usual" mentality that often leads to mediocre accomplishments. Using benchmarks may issue a sharp wake-up call to organizations that have lulled themselves to sleep by thinking they are unique.

Often an organization will decide to adapt a survey from a publication or one used by another organization. Usually this step is to create a unique survey for the organization. Part of the reasoning for such an approach is thinking that the organization is unlike any other and must have a survey that is reflective of the uniqueness of the particular organization. There is a fatal flaw in this line of reasoning. A unique organization denies the opportunity for comparison and such a stance is unrealistic. All organizations share some common properties, and real advantages accrue to being able to compare these properties with other organizations. A colleague of mine, Mark Yudof, spoofs this kind of parochial reasoning in academic organizations by calling this condition MUTE (Militant University Transcendental Exceptionalism).[1] This conceptual error denies the organization the opportunity to learn from other organizations. It fails to apprehend that no property can be evaluated if a background or context is unavailable. A person is only young or old relative to someone else. A new Ford is a quality auto only as compared with some other auto. To be truly useful, any assessment of organizational properties must obtain some comparison or benchmark values. One of the important strengths of the SOE is the wide range of comparisons or benchmarks that are available through its database of user organizations.

However, since every organization also has its unique aspects as well as its own specific history, it is important to be able to develop quantitative information about such specifics. The SOE permits each organization to develop a battery of customized questions that can be efficiently distributed with the standardized questions. This chapter provides information about how elements can be varied to customize SOE information to the particular needs of each organization.

Issues of Validity and Reliability

When any instrument is created, two questions must be considered.[2] First, does the instrument, regularly and dependably, provide measures of the underlying phenomena? For example, does the measure provide approximately the same information on a Monday as it does on a Tuesday of the same week with no other changes occurring in what is being measured other than the passage of a day? This property is called reliability. Several techniques exist to examine the degree of reliability. These include experimental designs that vary the presentation order of questions in an instrument, taking measures of similar groups of persons at different times, and statistical tools that examine the degree of consistency within an instrument. Cronbach's "alpha" coefficient is the best known of these tools. During pre-testing development of the SOE, various statistical tests were performed to achieve an appropriate level of reliability for each question and for the entire instrument. Additional attention was paid to the length of time required to complete the instrument and the required reading level of each question as well as issues of alternative meaning that some words and phrases may have. Pre-test data indicated that the SOE provides reliable measures (Cronbach's alpha of .85 or greater) for the scales of employee attitudes and employee information and that most respondents can complete the instrument in thirty minutes or less.[3]

The second question is this: does the instrument actually measure what it is intended to measure? This is the general concern of the validity of the instrument. The SOE in its continual development addresses validity concerns in a variety of ways. One is to compare findings with other measures to determine whether there is a convergence in findings. Comparisons with tools such as Likert's Five Systems,

Dean's Alienation Scale, and Maslach's Burnout Inventory indicate predicted levels of convergence on the various aspects of the SOE. A second means of establishing validity is to compare survey data to ratings by trained and seasoned observers. Limited inquiry along this dimension supports the findings of the SOE, though more will become known as information is acquired from longer-term studies now underway.

An important validity measure in the SOE is how valid the data appear to the survey's users—organization employees, organization leadership, and state leadership. For the organization, this question is one of how honest people were in taking the SOE. In our experience, people are quite candid in what they enter on the SOE. If they are suspicious, they simply refuse to take the SOE. It is important to remember that the underlying reason for using the SOE is not to obtain some descriptive profile of an organization that is then entered in a museum or registry. The underlying reason is to acquire internal data from the eyes of organizational membership of what membership thinks are strengths and weaknesses. These collective data then become the departure point for the organization in its efforts to improve. Thus, the most crucial test of both validity and reliability is whether the data are used by the organization and whether the organization takes steps toward continuous improvement.

Levels of Data Analysis

SOE data are compiled and returned to the organization once the data collection period has ended. The results provided to the organization are divided into two primary levels of analysis: individual survey items (survey questions) and Survey Constructs (see Appendix A for the 1998 SOE instrument).

Individual Survey Items

The SOE consists of five types of individual survey items:
- Primary items
- Over-time items
- Employment benefit items
- Customized survey questions
- Demographic questions

These items provide the most detailed level of analysis. The content of the questions is geared to reflect concerns from organizational literature (quality, effectiveness, teamwork, empowerment, innovation, commitment, etc.), trends in both the private and public sector addressing improving quality, and programs to increase employee dedication and involvement. Many questions were developed through input from organizational representatives, and the questions were subjected to extensive pilot testing in several Texas state agencies.

Primary Items

These survey questions make up the main body of the SOE instrument. Organizational members are asked to respond to these questions by indicating to what extent they agree or disagree with the statement as it relates to the whole organization. The second page of the survey instrument in Appendix A presents the primary items.

The average (arithmetic mean) score for these questions may range from a low of 1.0 (Strongly Disagree) to a high of 5.0 (Strongly Agree). Any question with an average mean score falling below the neutral midpoint of 3.0 indicates that, on average, employees perceive the issue more negatively than positively. Our usual experience is that *questions with scores below 2.0 should be a significant source of concern for the organization and receive immediate attention.* The standard deviation, response frequency count, and number of respondents for each question are included in the data report for these questions. At the bottom of page 3 of the SOE are items newly introduced in 1998. The items reflect concerns from participants that they wanted to distinguish their perceptions of their immediate work group from their perceptions of the total organization.

Over-Time Items

Another grouping of questions included in the SOE asks respondents to compare their perceptions of important organizational dimensions with those of two years ago. These items are on the fourth page of the SOE. This set of questions provides a historical perspective of change in the organization and is especially valuable for organizations participating in the SOE for the first time. Over-time items are also useful because they estimate the general direction of employee perceptions at a specific point in time. They readily indicate if employees perceive trends as toward improvement or deterioration over the previous two years. The section at the top of page 4 of the SOE (Appendix A) are the over-time items.

As with the primary items described above, the scoring methodology for these questions is based on the average (arithmetic mean) score, with the range of scores extending from a low of 1.0 (Strongly

Disagree) to a high of 5.0 (Strongly Agree). Scores falling below the neutral midpoint of 3.0 indicate that, on average, employees perceive the issue more negatively than positively. Again, our experience has been that *questions with scores below 2.0 should be a significant source of concern for the organization and receive immediate attention.* The standard deviation, response frequency count, and number of respondents are also included in the data report for these questions.

Employment Benefit Items

An important part of having a creative and effective workforce is providing benefits that support the needs of employees. Employment benefits have become a fundamental element of employment. This part of the compensation package significantly impacts workforce issues as complex as employee recruitment, retention, and morale, issues which factor heavily into the long-term success of the organization.

Due to the high costs associated with employment benefits and their significant impact on the workplace, organizations should routinely evaluate their benefit package to determine whether it continues to meet the needs of the workforce. Periodic examination of the benefit package ensures that the most appropriate benefits are offered to employees and that the organization receives the most effective return on its investment.

The SOE includes a series of questions about employment benefits. The questions ask employees to indicate their satisfaction with particular benefit items. The employment benefits included on the SOE's questionnaire are commonly found in many organizations, though not all will be found in every organization. In addition to providing information about employee benefit satisfaction, these questions also enable organizations to determine how preferences for specific employment benefits may be affected by employee attributes, such as age, gender, and ethnicity.

Customized Survey Questions

While the SOE gathers data about a variety of organizational issues, many organizations find it valuable to add questions to the survey instrument that will address issues unique to the organization. What employees think about issues such as recent organizational changes or agency-wide training initiatives are often measured with customized questions.

Organizations may submit as many as twenty customized questions to be included in the SOE. These questions are included in the

SOE insert and are mailed only to employees of the specific organization. Each question may include up to six possible responses.

Developing customized questions for the SOE presents an opportunity to involve persons from different parts of the organization in the survey process. These questions are an efficient means for the organization to gather information that may be needed by various areas of the organization.

Here are some guidelines to consider when designing customized survey questions:

Questions should be phrased positively. For example, a question designed to elicit employees' perceptions of cultural diversity training should be written as follows: "Cultural diversity training is making this organization a better place to work" (as opposed to "Cultural diversity training has not made a difference in this organization").

Questions should be applicable to all employees. Each employee filling out a survey should be able to respond to every question. If it is necessary to include questions that may not apply to all employees, include a "Don't Know/Not Applicable" response category.

Only one issue should be addressed in each survey question. For example, a survey question written as "The alternative work schedule policy has improved employee morale and reduced burnout" asks about two issues—morale *and* burn-out. This question should be divided into two questions to yield the most useful and unambiguous data for the organization.

Customized questions send a message to employees about what is important to management. When considering whether to include customized questions, or when designing these questions, keep in mind that the subject(s) addressed in the questions will communicate to employees what is important to the management of the organization. Regardless of how employees respond to these questions, they can serve to set a particular tone for the organization or to communicate certain priorities.

Appendix B contains examples of customized questions, some of which have been written by organizations participating in previous surveys.

Demographic Questions

The fifth type of question included in the SOE is demographic. These questions offer the organization a detailed look into the composition of the workforce, including employee attributes such as gender, ethnicity, age, and education. Some of the demographic questions offer information not usually gathered in human resource offices, such as how many persons are in the employee's household and what the employee's economic role in the household may be. Important issues may reside in these questions about the relative importance of benefits and whether there are additional wage earners in the household.

The data that result from these questions are informative in themselves because they provide a detailed picture of the workforce, such as whether it is becoming older, more ethnically diverse, or more educated. However, these data may be even more useful when cross-tabulated with other survey results. When survey results are sorted by demographic criteria, the data provide insight into whether factors such as gender, ethnicity, age, and income influence employee perceptions. For example, do women view organizational issues differently than men do? Or do younger employees have views of pay and benefits than differ from those of older employees? Appendix B provides an illustration of how an organization may add demographic variables.

Consistent with survey procedures, demographic information is not returned to the organization if there are fewer than five respondents in any category. This is designed to protect employees' anonymity (the first page of the 1996–1997 SOE instrument in Appendix A shows the demographic questions included in the SOE).

A Look at the Texas State Government Workforce: Demographic Information

If 1994–1995 SOE results are generalized to the rest of the workforce, the following conclusions can be drawn about the Texas state government workforce:

75 percent of all state employees grew up in Texas.

85 percent of all state employees expect to be working for their organization for at least the next two years.

66 percent of all state employees are the primary wage earner in their household, and 60 percent live in households where there is more than one wage earner.

The median gross income earned by a state employee falls between $23,001 and $27,000.

Employees between the ages of 40 and 49 make up the largest segment of the workforce.

Almost half (48 percent) of the state's workforce has a bachelor's or graduate degree.

Reporting SOE Results

The information presented in this chapter should provide organizations with the basic tools necessary to understand and interpret SOE data for the purposes of data analyses and reporting. However, many other data combinations and comparisons are available for interpreting SOE data. For instance, many organizations use SOE data to take an in-depth look across divisions, departments, programs, or even job functions. Others use SOE data to make external comparisons to organizations that may be similar or that represent important benchmarks.

Internal Comparisons

Data comparisons within the organization highlight the extent to which employee perceptions are consistent throughout the organization at a specific point in time or over longer time periods. Several options are available for internal data comparisons, including analysis by organizational categories, cross-tabulated comparisons, and internal comparisons over time.

Analysis by Organizational Categories

Organizations have the option of tailoring the survey instrument to facilitate specific internal comparisons. SOE respondents may be asked to identify up to two workplace categories in which they belong. (Organizational category breakdowns are not recommended for organizations with fewer than fifty employees.) Data from these categories make it possible to understand the viewpoints of employees from different parts of the organization and to determine the extent to which perceptions may or may not be consistent throughout the organization. These data are also helpful for many managers who want to use results specific to their office or division in localized improvement efforts.

Results for each survey question are provided for every organizational category submitted *unless the category contains fewer than five respondents.* Therefore, organizations should not isolate employee groups that contain fewer than twenty-five or thirty persons in order to ensure that data will be returned for each category.

Organizational categories should be somewhat broad and designed so that they will produce meaningful data for the organization. Response options under each category should be mutually exclusive; employees should identify with *only one* option under each organizational category. Some of the most common organizational categories include employees' regional location and job function.

Examples of some possible organizational categories are shown in Appendix B.

Cross-tabulated Results

As previously mentioned, survey results may be cross-tabulated with other survey data to provide a detailed look at the perceptions of certain employee groups. Demographic questions are commonly used for these types of comparisons. For instance, if an organization wants to find out how African-American employees perceive managers' incorporation of cultural diversity in the workplace, the score for the survey question "Managers are committed to incorporating cultural diversity" would be isolated for all African-American respondents.

Comparisons over Time

The environment is constantly changing, and part of being a successful organization means finding ways to anticipate and to adapt to these changes. One of the significant advantages of regular SOE participation is the opportunity to measure how the organization has adapted to the environment and changed over time. Organizations that participate in each replication of the SOE, in effect, produce a unique history of the organization that highlights areas of growth and provides clues as to issues that may be problematic in the future. This historical perspective becomes a valuable, data-driven record of organizational growth, establishing the impact of changes in areas of leadership, resources, and new mandates, to name only a few.

Over-time comparisons are an important aspect of the SOE. Nevertheless, at times it is necessary to make changes in the instrument to capture issues of new importance or to eliminate dated language used in the instrument. In these instances, direct mathematical comparisons from year to year will be affected.

External Comparisons

External comparisons, especially benchmarking, have become important business practices in recent years in both private and public organizations. In short, the concept involves identifying a need within the organization, determining what other organizations have done to address the problem ("best practices"), and adopting these practices to meet the need of the organization. The SOE assists organizations in seeking to develop benchmarks by providing a series of external comparisons about many different kinds of workplace issues.

Data from the SOE can be used to assist organizations in establishing benchmarks for many different aspects of organizational functioning. Human resources policies, such as alternative work schedules, are one example. The SOE indicates whether employees perceive the existence of such schedules. Inferences then can be made on what effects such policies have on the workforce.

Flexible work schedule policies have emerged as one of the most recommended business strategies to help organizations reduce stress and burn-out in the workplace. Programs such as compressed work weeks, job sharing, and flex-time have become popular among employees who must balance work and home responsibilities. They are also popular with many managers who praise them as a cost-neutral way to positively affect employees' working conditions while reducing lost work time.

As spotlighted in the April 1996 SOE newsletter, employees at the Texas Department of Insurance (TDI) report the most satisfaction with opportunities for flexible work schedules. TDI received the highest score (4.5) for the survey question "Alternative work schedules are offered to employees" among all fifty-two participating agencies.

Data reports like this can prevent organizations from "reinventing the wheel" when developing or revising organizational policies and processes. SOE data are used to identify best practices in Texas state government, as in the TDI example, and share information across organizations to further improvement endeavors.

External comparisons also provide organizations with benefits beyond formal benchmarking activities; these comparisons offer organizations a broader context by which to view their own survey data. For example, knowledge can be gained when an organization compares itself to similar entities in the area of employee job satisfaction. If the organization finds that it ranks the lowest overall among like organizations, this finding will undoubtedly offer a greater perspective in which to view to the organization's own data. It may indicate, among other things, that the organization will perhaps face higher employee turnover than its competitors, or the quality of work and service will suffer, resulting in lost customers or dissatisfied clients.

In effect, broad external comparisons enrich the meaning of the data for the organization by establishing a "norm" for groups of organizations, helping organizations to set goals and, conversely, helping organizations determine areas of real accomplishment and strength.

Statewide Averages

One of the most beneficial elements of the SOE is the opportunity to acquire information about employee perceptions in many different kinds of organizations. With more than 70,000 surveys distributed in the 1996–1997 administration of the SOE for the state of Texas, a variety of data are available. The available information includes how employees perceive their employing organizations as a whole and, in the case of state organizations, the state as their employer. These data are referred to as the statewide averages and are determined by averaging the responses of SOE respondents from all organizations. The statewide average scores provide a very popular context by which organizations evaluate their own results.

The statewide data set provided to organizations is a compilation of all SOE respondents. In direct comparisons of organizations that vary greatly in size (number of respondents), larger organizations will likely evince a statistical tendency to regression to the mean or midpoint of the scale. Smaller organizations may conversely have a greater likelihood of achieving very low or very high scores.

This statistical probability has special implications, especially for larger organizations, because extreme scores (high or low) are more difficult to achieve. Therefore, when extreme scores occur in larger organizations, the data affirm that there is a significant consensus in perceptions. Consequently, when the score for a particular topic is very high in large organizations, one may conclude that most employees perceive that topic as a *significant* strength for the organization. Conversely, very low scores *strongly* imply that these issues should be viewed as areas where most employees have great concern.

Comparisons with Other Organizations

One of the significant strengths of the SOE is the broad range of organizations that can be used as a basis for comparisons. Utilization of the SOE by organizations in other states, local governments, private not-for-profit organizations, and private businesses means that many meaningful and often critical comparisons can be made. When employees or board members ask questions about how the organization compares in terms of wages, benefits, or employee attitudes, the diverse set of organizational benchmarks make such questions readily answerable.

Available Results Formats

Survey results are delivered to the organization in a variety of formats designed to expedite delivery and to facilitate utilization. The formats include a hard-copy report, data diskette, and results reported via the Internet.

Formal Report

The hard-copy report is the traditional format for presenting SOE results. Currently, it is the most comprehensive of the formats, outlining all survey results and containing descriptive narrative on potential organizational interventions. The report is designed to allow organizations to reproduce additional copies for greater distribution.

Disk

Survey data are also returned to the organization in a computer-readable disk. This enables organizations to manipulate data for special reporting purposes, such as graphing or other display needs. Both organization and statewide results are provided on the diskette.

Internet Accessibility

One of the important functions of the SOE is to make data continuously available to all participating organizations, including state executive and legislative entities. It is also important for employees to be able to get information routinely about their organization and similar organizations. One of the challenges of building organizations that can rapidly respond to environmental change is finding modalities to transmit information rapidly and economically. The emerging preeminent modality is the Internet.

Progress Underway

Internet publishing of limited public portions of these data is an economical and efficient means of meeting that responsibility. Aspects of administering the SOE via the Internet are in use by some organizations, and such technologies loom large as both alternative and expanded tools for distributing information within an organization and to other organizations.

Consequently, substantial efforts have been directed toward publishing some of the SOE data on the Internet as well as collecting data directly via HTML forms. In the next few years much of the current pencil-and-paper-based technology of gathering employee opinions will be replaced by Internet technologies. Just as scanned forms replaced clerks reading questionnaires and keypunching data into cards to feed into computers, the Internet will permit direct collection of the data and rapid compilation of results. The emerging Internet technologies have great potential for every organization. They carry the promise of far greater levels of effective communication within organizations and the likelihood that organizations will be transformed into structures far different from where many of us work today.

Current Modes of SOE Data Availability

Data provided on the Internet includes a narrative file to frame the human resource issues faced by each organization at the time of the survey and general data summaries for the SOE's twenty constructs. In order to maintain the assurances of individual respondent anonymity, the raw data of each individual questionnaire and all of an organization's data are not available on the Internet. The data summaries provided offer the information necessary for organizations to do organization-to-organization comparisons and larger comparisons to a variety of averages. Data from the surveys are typically available to survey liaisons via e-mail attachments.

The SOE data and various additional facts can be accessed at this World Wide Web address: *http://www.utexas.edu/depts/sswork/survey/*. This location provides data from the various surveys of organizations over the years as well as data from the current survey for a given organization. Links are provided to the Web pages maintained by each organization and by the Texas Department of Information Resources as well as many other Internet resources.

The construction of the Web pages, the HTML protocols, can be accessed by recent versions of either Netscape Navigator or Microsoft's Internet Explorer. Standards change quickly on the Internet, and as of this date these are the preferred tools for traversing the World Wide Web. Because of graphic content, pages in many instances will be most easily read from a site with a T1 line or similar fast access. Downloadable files, such as SOE newsletters and special survey reports, are in Microsoft Word or Excel format. These are widely used word processor and spreadsheet applications, and state site licenses are available for Texas agencies. Graphic-intensive reports that require sophisticated page layout software are available as PDF files. PDF is a proprietary file convention of the page layout software Pagemaker, a product of Adobe Corporation. Free software for viewing and printing PDF files is available from the Adobe site. In time, most data releases will be moved fully to the Internet to increase the speed and availability of access.

SOE Data and Organizational Improvement

Organizational cultures play a significant role in both organizational effectiveness and customer satisfaction. Appropriate organizational cultures are thus critical to organizational survival and success. However, problems arise because it is very difficult to determine systematically what an organization's culture looks like. Moreover, building appropriate organizational cultures requires two more steps that are challenging: to define what issues in the culture should be a concern for leadership and what should be done to improve them.

The SOE provides a means to turn many "soft" issues into quantifiable measures of change, highlighting progress and areas that may be weaknesses. While this chapter has provided the information needed to understand the data presented in the SOE reports, the real purpose of any employee attitude survey is to apply the data and generate improvements. Even organizations whose data reveal much strength face this challenge of continuously improving. As the old line among coaches goes, "Becoming number one is easier than remaining number one."

Summary

This chapter covers the general construction of questions in the SOE and how data generated by the SOE are provided to participating organizations. The next chapter details how the questions from the SOE are used to develop specific concepts that describe organizations and provide directions for interventions to improve organizations. The chapter expands these concepts with specific illustrations to assist persons charged with administering organizations or persons holding the responsibility of achieving change in an organization. The material presented draws from the practical experiences of hundreds of managers working to improve organizational performance and the growing theoretical frameworks and empirical studies available from the behavioral and social sciences.

4 | Procedures for Organizational Assessment and Intervention

The steps taken to promote improvements in the organization are the most critical part of any organizational assessment. Organizations are not like a block of wood or slab of iron that only changes when a specific action is taken. All organizations are, to some degree, in a state of continuous flux. They are interacting with the environment at the same time they are being changed by interactions among members of the organization. The very act of involving the entire workforce in an attitude survey or human resource assessment is a very powerful and comprehensive intervention in itself. A regularly scheduled survey sends a message that employee input is a constant and critical data benchmark by which to measure organizational progress. The use of a scheduled survey is a simple and direct acknowledgment of the continuous change that characterizes any organization and serves as a path to guide those changes toward desired goals.

When an organization follows the processes described in this book and shares survey results with its membership, actively encourages feedback from employees, and implements improvements based on this input, it moves toward goals of excellence and quality. The SOE serves as a compass, a direction finder that engages leadership and employees in focused dialogues to define problems and achieve solutions.

Intervention Assessment

Any kind of measurement should be tied to some larger purpose or use. Here is an example. Once a physician measures a person's blood pressure, the measurement should include some corollary information that tells the physician and the patient about aspects of the patient's health relative to blood pressure. If the measurement indicates problems, then related interventions need to be identified.

Surveys in organizations should be taken with a similar intent. They should be used to find strengths and weaknesses in the organization and to establish procedures for improving the organization. While it is easy to pose inquiries to organizational members, it is more difficult to create questions that identify specific problems and to take the steps that may resolve them. This chapter should assist organizations participating in the SOE to gain a better understanding of the organization's strengths and weaknesses as detected by the survey. This assessment is intimately tied to the evolution of this survey; it clarifies the link between the scores on the SOE report and the issues affecting the organization. It likewise provides suggestions for improving specific weakness in the organization.

We can group organizational life by five broad categories.[1] These categories help leadership and all members of the organization assess its strengths and weaknesses.

One aspect of organizational life is working in face-to-face groups. Employees come into direct contact with each other and with their supervisors in this aspect. This is called the *Work Team*. The SOE offers assessments to determine how effective work teams are. This is the first organizational dimension derived from the survey questions.

A second aspect of organizational life concerns the physical working conditions and the monetary and related rewards that the employee receives from the organization. This dimension is termed *Work Settings/Accommodations*. The SOE assesses the degree to which organizational members perceive that they have the tools to do their jobs and whether the rewards are appropriate and fair.

A third dimension of organizational life deals with the goals, vision, and mission of the organization and is called *General Organizational Features*. What does the organization stand for? What is the organization seeking to do, to accomplish? The SOE quantifies how organizational members rate the organization in terms of its goals, vision, and mission.

A fourth dimension of organizational life is how communication occurs within the organization and to the outside. This is termed *Communication Patterns*. From one viewpoint, an organization is simply information and the transfer of information. A manufacturing organization uses information about customer needs and information about how to transform raw materials to produce an item that meets customer needs. Service and governmental organizations are information-intensive entities that acquire data, convert the data to information, and make it available to clients and customers. The SOE provides assessments from organizational members about how well these tasks are handled.

A fifth dimension of organizational life examines the degree of "wear and tear" that employees face in their jobs. This is called *Personal Demands*. The reality of modern life is that employees have a heavy physical and emotional investment in their jobs. Work is often an important anchor in life, or even the major one, and has a great impact upon the family and community involvement of the worker. The SOE provides summary information about how employees are faring relative to the psychological demands of the work environment.

These five dimensions—Work Team, Work Settings/Accommodations, General Organizational Features, Communication Patterns, and Personal Demands—provide a major set of concepts wherein problems can be identified and remedies created. Within these five dimensions are twenty subcategories of target issues called constructs. An example of a construct is Supervisor Effectiveness. This construct directly assesses how well employees feel they are supervised. The five dimensions and the twenty constructs are the primary building blocks of organizational assessment and interventions.

Constructs lead directly to visible characteristics of the organizations. The Problem Manifestations tied to each construct in the intervention assessment are examples of the behaviors that may be manifested in the organization when the related construct is found problematic. These examples provide further elaboration of the construct.

The Interventions provided with each construct serve as the starting point for organizational members to discuss possible improvement activities. However, organizational cultures are both complex and unique, and therefore successful intervention strategies do not necessarily transfer from one organization to another. This underscores the importance of involving employees as much as possible when designing improvements to determine what employees think will be successful in their own work environment. By involving employees, the organization is also more likely to secure their "buy in" and personal commitment for change.

Dimension I: Work Team

This dimension relates to employees' activities with others in their immediate vicinity and concerns how the employee interacts with peers, supervisors, and all of the persons most closely involved in their day-to-day work activity. The constructs included in this dimension are Supervisor Effectiveness, Fairness, Team Effectiveness, Job Satisfaction, and Diversity.

Construct 1: Supervisor Effectiveness

This construct provides insight into the nature of supervisory relationships in the organization, including the quality of communication, leadership, thoroughness, and fairness that employees perceive between supervisors and themselves.[2] This construct helps organizational leaders determine the extent to which supervisory relationships are a positive element of the organization. A low score on the construct might suggest that training on supervisory skills may be needed to align more closely these relationships with the mission and desired values of the organization.

Problem Manifestations

Employees are concerned that work does not meet high standards or relate effectively to what is expected by customers and clients. High costs and doubts about effectiveness of activities exist. Data on job performance are usually not available. Employees feel that supervision is not focused on work but instead on other inappropriate criteria. Management insists that services and products are unique and there are no comparable services or products, thus denying needed efforts to establish external benchmarks.

Interventions

Train supervisors.
Examine how supervisors are selected.
Closely tie supervisory conferences to organizational goals and individual job tasks.

Establish career development procedures for supervisory and management development.

Develop internal evaluation tools.

Related Survey Questions

Work groups receive adequate feedback that helps improve their performance.

Employees have an opportunity to participate in the process of strategic planning and goal setting.

Employees seem to be working toward the same goals.

Each employee is given the opportunity to be a leader.

Employees are given accurate feedback about their performance.

Management knows whether an individual employee's life goals are compatible with organizational goals.

People who challenge the status quo are valued.

Promotion recommendations are made by a team of evaluators.

Raises and promotions are designed to ensure that workers are rewarded solely for their performance.

Construct 2: Fairness

This construct measures the extent to which employees perceive that a level playing field exists for all members of the organization and that performance is judged by fair, open, and job-based criteria.

Problem Manifestations

Employees feel promotion decisions are not based on performance. "Good ol' boy" and "good ol' girl" networks are seen as the predominant way by which advancement occurs. Open examination and thinking are not encouraged. Only one person speaks for the organization, and individual employees are stifled in attempts to assume greater responsibility. A forceful and willful leader and cautious followers characterize the organization; or no one seems to be in charge.

Interventions

Promote organizational cultural change toward participation and openness.

Establish quality teams to openly examine goals and procedures and recommend improvements.

Make data available to clearly explain how people are given assignments and promotions.

Train supervisors in speaking openly and candidly with employees.

Related Survey Questions

Average work is rewarded the same as excellent work.

There is a basic trust among employees and management.

Alternative work schedules (flex-time, compressed work weeks, job sharing) are offered to employees.

Raises and promotions are designed to ensure that workers are rewarded solely for their performance.

Construct 3: Team Effectiveness

This construct captures employees' perceptions of the people within the organization that they work with on a daily basis to accomplish their jobs (the work group or team).[3] This construct gathers data about how effective employees think their work group is as well as the extent to which the organizational environment supports cooperation among employees.

Problem Manifestations

There is a lack of cooperation among employees and evidence of gossip and conflict. People prefer to work alone; to the customer, it seems as if "the right hand does not know what the left hand is doing." There are many meetings and teams, but nothing seems to get accomplished.

Interventions

Train in teamwork.

Redesign work to permit teams to define work procedures, output measures, etc.

Structure performance evaluations to support work team results.

Related Survey Questions

Work groups receive adequate feedback that helps improve their performance.

Decision making and control are given to employees doing the actual work.

There is a basic trust among employees and management.

Employee productivity is high.

We "walk our talk."

Construct 4: Job Satisfaction

This construct looks at the degree to which employees intrinsically like their jobs and the total work environment. It focuses on both the job itself and the availability of resources to do the job.

Problem Manifestations

Employees express dissatisfaction with work and the organization. Low levels of quality and employee dedication to tasks exist. When asked about the job, employees discuss the employment benefits rather than a sense of mission and accomplishment concerning work. There is high employee turnover and absenteeism. Exit interviews indicate dissatisfaction with work as a reason for leaving.

Interventions

Restructure jobs and provide enrichment.

Allow job sharing and rotation.

Create opportunities to learn about other jobs in the organization.

Involve employees in defining objectives for their jobs.

Develop greater supervisory skills in assigning work and understanding demands faced by employees.

Related Survey Questions

Employees have adequate resources to do their job.

The environment supports a balance between work and personal life.

The pace of work in this organization enables employees to enjoy their work.

Construct 5: Diversity

This construct addresses the extent to which employees feel that personal differences, including ethnicity, social class, or lifestyle, may result in alienation from the larger organization and missed opportunities for learning or advancement. It examines the extent to which the organization understands and uses diversity in the workforce to relate to a complex culture and uses creativity arising from individual differences to improve organizational effectiveness.

Problem Manifestations

There is limited representation in the organization by ethnicity, gender, geographical, or socioeconomic background. Members of the organization have difficulty relating to different people and different areas of the state. Creativity is lacking because there is little diversity in members' backgrounds and experiences. The organization has irregular representation of various groups throughout sections and levels of the organization ("chiefs" and "Indians" come from different "tribes"). Leadership is not a mix of persons who rise from within the organization and persons who come from the outside.

Interventions

Target recruitment procedures and training programs for persons that are underrepresented to improve size of candidacy pools for promotion.

Conduct community outreach, including recruitment programs with high schools and colleges.

Establish mentor programs to encourage the development of opportunities for underrepresented groups.

Related Survey Questions

My close contacts and coworkers are a lot different from people elsewhere in the organization.

Every employee is valued.

Managers are committed to incorporating cultural diversity.

Work groups (that group of people with whom you have daily contact) are trained to incorporate the opinions of each member.

Dimension II: Work Settings/Accommodations

This dimension looks at the physical work setting and the factors associated with compensation, work technology, and tools. It covers concerns not only about the adequacy of offices, office equipment, and location but also about employment benefits. It includes information on the extent to which the organization recognizes the need to continuously develop the knowledge and skills of employees. This is what the organization brings to the table; it is the "total benefits package" provided to employees. The constructs included in this dimension are Fair Pay, Adequacy of Physical Environment, Benefits, and Employment Development.

Construct 6: Fair Pay

This construct addresses perceptions of the overall compensation package offered by the organization. It describes how well the compensation package holds up when employees compare it with those of similar jobs in other organizations.

Problem Manifestations

Employees complain that pay is inadequate to work expectations and demands. Employees feel they do not have the ability to maintain a standard of living similar to that offered by comparable work in other organizations. There is employee unrest about wages and benefits, resulting in high turnover and high levels of employee complaints.

Interventions

Increase pay.

Conduct wage comparison studies to determine whether unfair pay standards exist.

Provide increased employment benefit education.

Develop and communicate clearly defined policies for raises and promotions.

Show that management openly recognizes such complaints.

Related Survey Questions

Salaries are competitive with similar jobs in the community.

Benefits are comparable to those offered in other jobs.

Construct 7: Adequacy of Physical Environment

This construct captures employees' perceptions of the total work atmosphere and the degree to which employees believe that it is a "safe" working environment. This construct addresses the "feel" of the workplace as perceived by the employee.

Problem Manifestations

The office layout, desks, telephones, copiers, and computers are inadequate. Employees feel cramped and lack privacy. Customers and clients leave the organization feeling as if their dignity and confidentiality have been compromised. Parking, transportation, and the neighborhood present problems for employees. Employees fear for their personal safety within the building or in the neighborhood of the work site. Hazardous or potentially hazardous substances, machines, or working conditions exist. Employee creativity is stifled because of a lack of tools and resources. The conduct of supervisors is such that employees feel at risk.

Interventions

Acquire new space and technologies.

Change physical layout and utilization.

Develop programs that promote the sense of community within the organization, such as employee safety committees or other community projects.

Adhere to careful and rigorous selection, training, and supervision of supervisors.

Related Survey Questions

Employees have adequate computer resources (hardware and software).

Employees feel safe working in this organization.

Employees feel that they work in pleasant surroundings.

There is a feeling of community within this organization.

Construct 8: Benefits

This construct provides a good indication of the role the benefits package plays in attracting and retaining employees in the organization. It reflects comparable benefits that employees feel exist with other organizations in the area.

Problem Manifestations

The benefits package (health care, vacation, retirement, etc.) is seen as inadequate and inflexible. Certain important benefit items are missing, or items are too costly.

Interventions

Alter benefits plan.

Improve employee understanding of benefits.

Educate employees about how benefits relate to other community and governmental supports, such as social agencies, Social Security, personal savings, etc.

Related Survey Questions

Benefits can be selected to meet individual needs.

Benefits are comparable to those offered in other jobs.

The overall benefits and compensation packages offered by my employer were a consideration for me to take this position.

Construct 9: Employment Development

This construct is an assessment of the priority given to employees' personal and job growth. It provides insight into whether the culture of the organization sees human resources as the most important resource or as one of many resources. It directly addresses the degree to which the organization is seeking to maximize gains from investment in employees.

Problem Manifestations

There is a personnel function in the organization but not a development function. People do not learn new skills or secure additional educational development. Outmoded technologies are characteristically used. There is limited vertical or horizontal mobility in the organization. Supervisors and the organization do not develop career paths for employees. There are few opportunities for employee advancement, and higher-performing employees must jump to other employers to receive recognition. There is low investment in training and the acquisition of technology to improve job performance.

Interventions

Provide training programs.

Develop career ladders for employees.

Strengthen ties between organizational strategies and procedures for developing employees.

Post internal jobs.

Ensure fair access to internal positions.

Identify and use training programs, external education resources, membership and attendance at professional programs, trade events, etc.

Related Survey Questions

Work groups (that group of people with whom you have daily contact) are trained to incorporate the opinions of each member.

Training is made available to employees so that they can do their job better.

Employees have access to information about job opportunities, conferences, workshops, and training.

Management knows whether an individual employee's life goals are compatible with organizational goals.

Dimension III: General Organizational Features

This dimension captures the organization's interface with external influences. It is an internal evaluation of an organization's ability to assess changes in the environment and the quality of relations with customers, clients, or constituents. This dimension includes the general principles and values of the organization—the corporate culture. Many organizational characteristics play a role in this dimension. The characteristics include the degree and type of hierarchy that exists in the organization and the extent to which the work environment stresses employees' continuous learning, innovation, and creativity. It reflects as well the degree to which these characteristics are uniformly held throughout the organization. The constructs included in this dimension are Change Oriented, Goal Oriented, Holographic (Consistency), Strategic Orientation, and Quality.

Construct 10: Change Oriented

This construct secures employees' perceptions of the organization's capability and readiness to change based on new information and ideas. It addresses the organization's aptitude to process information timely and act upon it effectively. This construct also examines the organization's capacity to draw upon, develop, and utilize the strengths of all in the organization for improvement.

Problem Manifestations

The organization is reactive rather than proactive. Frequent organizational changes are done to avoid facing real problems. The organization is a band that can play only one song. It is characterized mainly by traditional ways of doing things. Change comes only when a crisis occurs.

Interventions

Provide training for top leadership.
Practice benchmarking with outside organizations.
Develop procedures to bring in "new blood" and new ideas.

Related Survey Questions

This organization integrates information and acts intelligently upon that information.

We routinely use different people from different parts of the organization to solve problems.

65

Employees have an opportunity to participate in the process of strategic planning and goal setting.

New ideas suggested by employees are seriously considered for implementation.

Creativity and innovation in work are encouraged.

Construct 11: Goal Oriented

This construct examines the extent to which the organization has clear goals and a commitment to reach those goals. It addresses the organization's ability to include its members in focusing its resources toward accomplishing and exceeding goals.

Problem Manifestations

Much of the work does not seem purposive. Work activities do not seem to be directed toward accomplishment. Things are done a given way because "that is the way things have always been done." There is no zest or passion for achievement.

Interventions

Involve employees in goal-setting processes.

Tie employees' work to "big picture" goals through diagramming or process-mapping techniques.

Install and utilize functional budgeting techniques.

Involve employees in establishing performance standards and measures.

Related Survey Questions

Our goals are consistently met or exceeded.

This organization integrates information and acts intelligently upon that information.

Employees have an opportunity to participate in the process of strategic planning and goal setting.

We are efficient.

Employee productivity is high.

We "walk our talk."

Construct 12: Holographic (Consistency)

This construct, which borrows a term familiar to physicists and engineers, refers to the degree to which all actions of the organization "hang together" and are understood by all. It concerns employees' perceptions of the consistency of decision making and activity within the organization.

Problem Manifestations

There is a slow response to challenges from the organization and employees. People are known to say one thing and do another. Divisions of the organization exist largely independently and there is little synergy across divisions or offices. The organization talks a good game but plays a sorry one. Employees are guided by thoughts such as "Ours is not to reason why, ours is but to do or die."

Interventions

Bring about a change in leadership via training or assignment.

Promote activities for organizational culture change (e.g., team building, retreats to build group solidarity, activities to build common values, etc.).

Implement job rotation (horizontal and vertical movement within organization).

Establish more adequate communication tools (newsletters, bulletin boards, etc.).

Related Survey Questions

My close contacts and co-workers are a lot different from people elsewhere in the organization.

Information and knowledge are shared openly in this organization.

The work atmosphere encourages open and honest communication.

We routinely use different people from different parts of the organization to solve problems.

Employees know how their work impacts other employees in the organization.

Decision making and control are given to employees doing the actual work.

Employees feel a sense of pride when they tell people that they work for this organization.

Work in this organization feels like it is "coming together."

Employees feel that their efforts count.

The "buck stops here" describes how employees accept personal accountability.

There is a feeling of community within this organization.

Construct 13: Strategic Orientation

The construct reflects employees' thinking about how the organization responds to external influences that should play a role in defining the organization's mission, vision, services, and products. Implied in this construct is the ability of the organization to seek out and work with relevant external entities.

Problem Manifestations

The organization lacks vision. The focus is on the immediate as opposed to anticipating how community, state, and national changes will affect the organization and its products or services. The organization is viewed as a fortress by customers, clients, and the community.

Interventions

Develop customer surveys to gather data on how customers or clients perceive the organization.

Develop inter-organizational teams and projects.

Establish executive exchanges with similar and different organizations.

Establish a compact between the organization and its stakeholders (board members, associations, clients or customers, community).

Related Survey Questions

We are known for our customer service.

We know who our customers are.

We work well with other organizations.

We work well with our governing bodies (the legislature, the board, etc.).

We work well with the public.

We understand the state, local, national, and global economic issues that impact this organization.

Construct 14: Quality

This construct focuses on whether quality is a value held by the organizational culture and the extent to which employees feel that they have the resources needed to deliver it.

Problem Manifestations

There is low or irregular quality. There are high levels of customer or client complaints. The organization is devoid of enthusiasm. Problems are covered up. The organization has many spin artists and devotes scarce resources to keeping a Teflon cover rather than trying to address the fundamental causes of problems.

Interventions

Bring about a change in leadership via training or assignment.

Provide training in quality; create quality circles or other activities that improve the ability of organizational members to articulate quality dimensions in all activities.

Improve education and training of all employees.

Ensure that there is a direct link between those leading the quality effort and top leadership.

Related Survey Questions

We are known for our customer service.

We are constantly improving our services.

We produce high-quality work that has a low rate of error.

We know who our customers are.

We develop services to match our customers' needs.

Average work is rewarded the same as excellent work.

Work in this organization feels like it is "coming together."

Employees have adequate resources to do their job.

Dimension IV: Communication Patterns

The Communication Patterns dimension refers to how formalized and structured communication is within the organization and to outside groups. It examines the degree to which communication is directed to work concerns, focused and effective. The constructs included in this dimension are Internal Communication, Availability of Information, and External Communication.

Construct 15: Internal Communication

This construct captures the flow of communication within the organization from the top down, from the bottom up, and across divisions or departments. It addresses the extent to which communication exchanges are open and candid and move the organization toward goal achievement.

Problem Manifestations

Communication flows only from the top down through silos. There is a lot of paperwork to cover oneself. Information is used like a power tool. Management communicates with employees on a "need to know" basis only. Most conversations occur behind closed doors. Gossip and informal communication are where the answers are found.

Interventions

Provide training on interpersonal communication.
Map the flow of paperwork.
Implement teamwork activities on open communication.
Renew leadership commitment to openness.

Related Survey Questions

Computerized information is easily shared among divisions in this organization.
The right information gets to the right people at the right time.
Information and knowledge are shared openly in this organization.
The work atmosphere encourages open and honest communication.
Work groups receive adequate feedback that helps improve their performance.
Employees are given accurate feedback about their performance.

Construct 16: Availability of Information

This construct addresses the extent to which employees feel that they know where to get needed information and that they know how to use it after they get it.

Problem Manifestations

The information needed to do the job is not available. Forms and procedures are not readily available but require separate requests. Technology such as the telephone and filing systems, databases, computers, and networks are inadequate.

Interventions

Revamp and revise information-sharing procedures and technologies.
Start cross-functional teams to develop information-sharing procedures.

Develop indexes of persons and functions (organizational directory).

Improve employee orientation and training on the organization's functions.

Improve ability of departments within the organization to communicate functions to others outside the department.

Make forms, policies, and procedures available on a computer network.

Related Survey Questions

Computerized information is easily shared among divisions in this organization.

The right information gets to the right people at the right time.

Employees feel that they must always go through channels to get their work done.

We understand the state, local, national, and global economic issues that impact this organization.

Employees know how their work impacts other employees in the organization.

Construct 17: External Communication

This construct looks at how information flows into the organization from external sources and, conversely, how information flows from inside the organization to external constituents. It addresses the ability of the organization's members to synthesize and apply external information to work performed by the organization.

Problem Manifestations

No effective or coordinated plan is in place to relate the organization's mission and goals to clients, policy makers, other agencies, and the public. Employees, in general, do not present a unified, clear, effective message of the organization's missions or goals.

Interventions

Design informational handouts.

Develop a speakers' bureau.

View every employee as an ambassador to the community.

Utilize technology (the media, the Internet, etc.) to communicate the organization's mission, goals, and programs.

71

Related Survey Questions

Computerized information is shared as appropriate with other organizations.

The work atmosphere encourages open and honest communication.

We work well with the public.

We understand the state, local, national, and global economic issues that impact this organization.

Employees have access to information about job opportunities, conferences, workshops, and training.

Dimension V: Personal Demands

This dimension reports on how much internalization of stress is occurring among employees. It provides information about the extent to which debilitating social and psychological conditions appear to be developing at the level of the individual employee. It addresses the important interface between employees' home and work lives and its impact on job performance and organizational efficiency. The constructs included in this dimension are Time and Stress Management, Burnout, and Empowerment.

Construct 18: Time and Stress Management

This construct looks at the extent to which employees feel that job demands are realistic, given time and resource limitations, and whether the work environment supports employees in balancing home and work demands. (The scoring methodology is maintained for this construct; the higher the score, the less likely time and stress management is a problem in the organization.)

Problem Manifestations

The workplace is stressful, with tempers often flaring. People end the day and the week exhausted. Manifestations of stress appear in personal lives through high rates of stress-related health problems (such as chronic infections, substance abuse, irritability, depression, etc.). Conflicts between home and work are frequent, increasing stress on employees. There is high utilization of sick leave. Employees are always reacting to crises rather than planning to prevent crises.

Interventions

Provide supervisory training to enable supervisors to more realistically schedule work and time demands.

Encourage better planning of work and work flow.

Rethink organizational structure and work assignment methods.

Offer alternative work schedules.

Related Survey Questions

Alternative work schedules (flex-time, compressed work weeks, job sharing) are offered to employees.

The environment supports a balance between work and personal life.

Employees balance their focus on both the long range and short term.

Construct 19: Burnout

This construct refers to a feeling of extreme mental exhaustion that negatively impacts employees' physical health and job performance, leading to lost organizational resources and opportunities.[4] (The scoring methodology is maintained for this construct; the higher the score, the less likely burnout is a problem in the organization.)

Problem Manifestations

Employees have low enthusiasm for work or for the accomplishments of the organization. Employees are not proud to work for the organization. Spontaneity, dedication, self-initiative, and creativity seem lacking. Involvement in community events is low. Employees blame others in the organization for problems and neglect personal accountability.

Interventions

Analyze job duties.

Reassign tasks.

Promote team building.

Counsel employees in aligning their expectations with organizational opportunities.

Related Survey Questions

Work in this organization feels like it is "coming together."

We "walk our talk."

Employees feel that their efforts count.

"The buck stops here" describes how employees accept personal accountability.

Creativity and innovation in work are encouraged.

Construct 20: Empowerment

This construct measures the degree to which employees feel that they have some control over their jobs and the outcome of their work. This construct provides a picture of how employees view the organizational structure—as a supportive, efficient environment or as one in which the formal and informal hierarchy hinders progress and innovation.

Problem Manifestations

Employees feel that they do not have the authority to do work and make needed changes. All employees must always go through channels to get work done. Employees fear punishment for pointing out mistakes or better ways of doing things. Customers must continuously contact persons at higher levels of authority to get problems solved. There are superfluous layers of supervision.

Interventions

Train supervisors.

Review how decisions are made throughout the organization.

Flatten the organizational structure.

Analyze management span of control to determine methods of greater delegation of power and responsibility.

Increase employee responsibility in identifying the best way to do their job.

Related Survey Questions

Employees feel that they must always go through channels to get their work done.

Employees know how their work impacts other employees in the organization.

Employees seem to be working toward the same goals.

There is a basic trust among employees and management.

Each employee is given the opportunity to be a leader.

Employees feel a sense of pride when they tell people that they work for this organization.

People who challenge the status quo are valued.

Summary

The SOE data have a number of uses. Data can be used simply to describe parameters of the workforce and of the organization. Such descriptive information is important to reflect how well trained and prepared the workforce is to be able to attain organizational goals. Indeed, one of the most dependable predictors of building quality in an organization is the extent to which education and training are a continuous part of the organization. Information from the SOE provides profiles that can be examined over time to assure that the organization is successful in developing a more highly educated workforce.

Additional steps in using the SOE results include using such descriptive information with other data such as interviews, focus groups, and professional consultation to set directions for organizational development. While every organization can readily develop the training to provide basic orientation to the organization and the job, programs to improve an organization require much more extensive and detailed knowledge of organizational properties and employee attitudes. Goals such as plans to increase creativity, enhance quality, deal with conflict creatively, and build sounder relations with clients and suppliers require detailed instruments and analyses. The five dimensions and the twenty constructs that are derived through the Intervention Assessment of the Survey establish precise procedures that permit an organization to focus on specific steps to improve organizational functioning.

Decisions about use of the data for interventions are the responsibilities of the organization's leaders, but efforts to bring change in the organization proceed most successfully when all employees are informed of changes and reasons for changes.

However, just presenting the data to all employees is not an adequate approach or the most advisable starting point. Rather, data need to be released and discussed to get employee affirmation of what the summaries present. Each respondent-employee knows only what he or she placed on the survey. The affirmation process is part of presenting the picture to the employees and establishing responsibility with all employees for the organization's current state, its strengths and weaknesses. Change and intervention decisions then flow from this important and essential step.

The next chapter provides some very specific procedures for using the data and material from the SOE. It focuses on the requisite tasks of leadership to use the information and to engage all members of the organization in improvement activities.

5 | Using the SOE in Changing the Organization

Organizations are created for several reasons. One is to acquire enough human energy and talent to achieve tasks that go beyond what one person or a few people can achieve. Another reason is to provide continuity beyond the lifetime of a single person. Many organizations appear very stable, and it is often assumed that organizations such as corporations and governments will simply last for the lifetime of many individuals. Such assumptions are often wrong, though. Any geographical atlas that is more than twenty years old will show a surprising instability of governments in Europe, Africa, or Asia. Business or corporations are equally short-lived. A recent study suggests that the average life expectancy of a multinational corporation is forty to fifty years.[1] In just a bit more than two decades, from 1970 to 1993, one-third of the companies listed in the *Fortune* 500 had disappeared—by being acquired, merged, or dissolved. The truly long-lived company is exceedingly rare.[2] Among the few exceptions are Stora, which began as a copper mine 700 years ago in Sweden, and Sumitomo, which originated as a copper-casting shop in 1590. The study suggests that much of their longevity has to do with the organizational metaphor through which these entities were developed.[3]

People have different views of organizations and assumptions about how an organization should work. Often we use metaphors to describe an organization, and the choice of metaphor implies how a person views organizations as a whole.

For some, an organization is a collection of people, a large family, where one works and interacts with others; typically, one gets along well with some co-workers and not as well with others. A person oriented to this metaphor expects affection and appreciation as well as loyalty and obedience from others. Good relations among people are important, as are observances of significant personal events such as holidays, birthdays, and anniversaries. Traditions of service, longevity of employment, and fidelity to organizational ideals are the most valued norms. Written job descriptions, employee performance contracts, and organizational charts are rare. In accord with this metaphor, such tools are viewed as destructive of the trust and reciprocity that are more essential to the organization. While organizations built upon this metaphor are capable of producing quality goods and services, it is difficult for the organization to grow beyond fifty or so employees. The organization may also be very resistant to change. When change does occur, it typically comes only from the top. Moreover, the upper levels of the organization may be quite isolated from many of the aspects of the organization's environment.

Each metaphor of organization seems to have its own special fallacy. Here it is the belief that everyone is in "one big, happy family." All too often jealousies, family secrets, and vendettas characterize these families.

For other persons, an organization is or should be a well-run and well-oiled machine, an army where orders are clear and issued from on high and where work gets done efficiently by each person fulfilling a discrete task. Managers issue directives crisply and expect them to be followed quickly. This is an organization where efficiency, clear chains of command, and discrete spans of control are prized. Written job descriptions, performance contracts for employees to guide supervision, and detailed work-monitoring and reporting procedures keep each person focused on work responsibilities. Such organizations achieve results by producing uniform products or services, often in great volume and for comparatively low costs. However, there is often little creativity in such organizations, and high turnover among employees is common. Work in these organizations can be frustrating to all but those in the highest echelons.

A central fallacy of this metaphor is the "professional manager" and the notion that employees can be viewed as components in a machine. This metaphor assumes that professional managers possess special skills on how to manage any organization. Leadership is simply seen as special training that tells one what kind of person to plug into a given job. But to the employee, often these professionals are viewed only as skilled manipulators, quick to jump to a higher post or better offer on the outside.

Another metaphor for an organization is a contentious neighborhood where different interest groups maneuver and collide with each seeking to secure resources and achieve a comparable advantage over competing groups. In this metaphor an organization is viewed as a political system. Success comes in isolating, competing groups and maintaining high solidarity within one's own group. Leadership will act to pit groups or divisions against each other and encourage an atmosphere of Darwinian competition based on the thinking that only the fit will survive. While such organizations may be creative, considerable energy is devoted to political infighting, and activities that require widespread collaboration are difficult to achieve. The results are that goods or services can be irregular in consistency and performance erratic over time.

This metaphor has two fallacies, "survival of the fittest" and "situational leadership." "Survival of the fittest" is a complex topic rooted in the work of Charles Darwin and seeks to explain why some members of a species and some species flourish and others die out. Modern evolutionary theory has moved much beyond these early notions as the concept of "fittest" has proven to be most complex. "Situational leadership," which until late was the runaway favorite of management theorists, recommends that leadership always be flexible and do what seems to work in the immediate term. Ends that justify any means and flexible leadership that is unanchored from principles in time leads to disintegration.

The Survey of Organizational Excellence is best used with the metaphor of an organization as a living, thinking entity—a learning or thinking organization. This is an organization where each person has a good sense of what the total purpose is, knows how his or her contributions serve organizational goals, and is eager to develop better ways of doing current tasks. Moreover, each individual is actively thinking about immediate challenges and long-term opportunities for the organization. The opportunity to participate provides an important reward for each employee, and the success of the organization itself contributes to greater employee security.

The most important strength of this metaphor of a thinking organization is its advantages in times of instability and change. The metaphor creates an organization that is rapidly responsive to the environment and that can change quickly to meet new challenges. Of all metaphors for organizations, this one is most likely to lead to success in highly fluid environments. Organizations that use such tools as the SOE are moving toward this organizational metaphor, the thinking organization. Such organizations have the promise of being the outstanding organizations of the future.

The fallacy in this metaphor is the trap of the "one best way" that proved so entrancing to the Scientific Management theorists. Such a fallacy is based upon the realization that at a given point of time there will likely be a best way of doing a given thing. Yet as time and opportunities change, the next best way can be different from today's best way. The promise of the thinking organization is to continually discover the best way.

Creating Outstanding Organizations

Visionary leadership creates outstanding organizations.[4] In turn, visionary leaders recognize that in order to be successful, they must have reliable data to guide decision making. These data must come from both those inside the organization, the employees, and those outside the organization, such as customers, clients, suppliers, and the public. The SOE is a prime source of information organized to provide a clear picture of internal functioning. It provides a variety of information that describes how employees feel about critical dimensions of the organization. It is most valuable when used to involve employees in continuously building improvements in the organization.

For all organizations there are several fundamental ingredients in using data to change and to build the kind of responsiveness to the environment and demands that characterize our times. With the return of the SOE data it is timely to review the following basic ingredients in organizational change:
- Moving from the Paradigm of Management to the Paradigm of Leadership
- Creating the Vision
- Communicating a Sense of Urgency
- Driving Fear Out
- Using Data as a Compass to Set the Direction and "Kick Start" Change
- Building the Change Team
- Choosing the Path and Goals

Essentials of Successful Change

These ingredients, when applied together, create a thinking organization that adapts to the environment, seizes opportunities, is responsive to the citizenry, and secures the loyalty and commitment of employees. The data from tools like the SOE are important aspects of two of these ingredients, Using Data as a Compass and Building the Change Team.

Moving from the Paradigm of Management to the Paradigm of Leadership

The use of tools such as the SOE signals the move of an organization from traditional reliance upon *management* orientations for getting results to applying a *philosophy of leadership*.

Traditional bureaucratic organizations are built upon principles that promote predictability and control. Explicit work rules, detailed reporting of activities, and supervision that seeks to control and direct efforts are all aspects of assembly-line management. Such traditional organizations are most successful in creating high-volume output with long production runs. Making thousands and thousands of copies of the same thing works well with this approach to creating and running an organization. In such organizations workers are supervised but not expected to think. Rather, they are to regularly and dependably perform a series of repetitive tasks. Indeed this is the sort of organization that engenders the employee credo "Ours is not to reason why; ours is but to do or die."

Achievement through Leadership, Not Command

If the challenge to the organization is to develop new products or services, to respond to a turbulent environment, to tailor complex services to a diverse clientele, and to continuously improve and innovate, then a very different organization is demanded. This is an organization not controlled through managers, but instead challenged by inspired leadership. This is a thinking organization.

The focus of this new paradigm or metaphor of the organization is on leadership. Leadership moves others not through command and control but through vision, example, integrity, candor, and consistency. It creates conditions of involvement through strong norms that demand the fullest exertion by all. Moreover, the only fear it causes its members is the fear that they are not making their greatest possible contribution. While some degree of the old paradigm of management, with its focus on order and control, will continue to be relevant, the emphasis in thinking organizations is changing to *leading, not managing, change.*

Digging Deep: The Use of Critique

Leadership means demanding that employees think and examine all dimensions to find a better way. It calls for everyone to *critique* all activities. When leadership is the organization norm, rather than management, every employee is called upon to fully use critique in examining every effort by the individual and the team. The goal of critique is to understand what a given task is, what it contributes to the final product, and how it might be improved. Using critique means to dig deep in every organizational process, shine light into each nook and cranny to increase understanding, build quality, and search relentlessly for a superior service or product. Every mistake, every shortcoming is not used as an excuse to blame but as an opportunity to build and improve.

Creating the Vision

Successful change comes only with visionary leadership.[5] The challenge of leadership today is to move organizations to a paradigm of excellence, participation, and innovation. The definition of successful leadership in today's organization starts with the articulation of a vision for the organization. The vision identifies where the organization is today and where it must go. Visions distinguish the organization from others and provide a special meaning and significance for all members.

Uniqueness is established first through the vision. Successful visions inspire followers, readily translate into concrete goals, and shatter complacency and laziness. Members of the organization come to define much of what they are through the vision. Such visions come from inspired leadership.

Communicating a Sense of Urgency

Allied with the creation of the vision is instilling a sense of urgency in everyone in the organization. Successful change cannot come without special sacrifice, strong exertion, and dedicated work. Complacency has many faces, includes attitudes of "business as usual" and jobs seen as entitlements. Cautious and uninspired supervisors control rather than enable and lead. "Don't make waves" is the order of the day. In organizations characterized by complacency, leaders simply preside and workers blithely assume that tomorrow will be much like today.

Moreover, the bearers of bad news that might challenge the status quo are labeled as malcontents. Organizational change demands considerable struggle. Until a sense of urgency is created, the necessary energy to propel organizational change is missing.

Part of the rationale for the SOE data is to lay the basis for building a sense of urgency by identifying areas where excellence is missing and creating action plans to improve those areas. Returning survey data to employees conveys the urgency to move forward by seeking out problems and promoting needed change.

Driving Fear Out

Coupled with creating a sense of urgency is creating conditions in which each member of the organization, each employee, is called upon to participate fully. To varying degrees, many organizations govern employees by fear. Threats of the loss of jobs, benefits, office resources, and the like are too often commonplace themes used to control and motivate employees. Warnings of downsizing, outsourcing, and reengineering can convey to the employee that he or she is a readily replaceable commodity. Supervisors using statements such as "my way or the highway" or "you need to learn to be a team player" can create high levels of fear and caution among employees. Urgency to contribute must be coupled with a sense that each person's contributions will be recognized and appreciated, and that employees need not fear reprisals resulting from honest mistakes or attempts to find better ways of getting work done. This is not a simplistic call for a climate of happy feelings and warm, fuzzy togetherness. This is a call for each person to participate fully and to challenge traditional bureaucratic ways of proceeding.

Visionary leadership must understand the dual and reciprocal nature of creating urgency and driving fear out. Creating urgency means conveying to all in the organization the highly competitive nature of existence and the need for continuous efforts of development and improvement. Driving fear out is learning to lead by incentives rather than controlling through threats. Employees of the thinking organization face and understand uncertainty with the sense of personal capability and teamwork skills to regularly confront and overcome ever larger challenges.

The next two ingredients of change are dependent upon some form of internal data. The SOE data are used as an internal data source for setting a compass direction for the organization and as material for initiating the activities of the Change Team. Specific suggestions are provided for implementing organizational change.

Using Data as a Compass to Set the Direction and "Kick Start" Change

The Survey of Organizational Excellence serves as a compass to set a direction for organizational change. It is a broad-based and dependable source of internal information about how an organization is functioning. The SOE data serve to set a direction and "kick start" the change process. Working with survey data suggests some important and useful ways of applying the findings to develop stronger, self-aware (learning) organizations.

For each employee these data represent a new viewpoint that may or may not correspond with the individual's attitudes. Each of us may feel that others agree with us, but until some type of survey is conducted, we cannot know for sure how representative our views are in relation to those of our colleagues. When these data are taken with external information from customers, clients, and competitors, they provide the organization with a critical assessment of current strengths and weaknesses. This information then readily indicates a path for improvement.

Identify Strengths and Weaknesses

When SOE results are returned, organizations are provided with data from each of the survey questions and twenty constructs derived from the questions. Start reviewing the data by examining responses to all sixty-five of the primary questions. Then sort the questions by those answers that have the highest average scores and those answers that have the lowest scores. This sorting provides an initial introduction to the areas in which employees feel the organization has its greatest strengths and weaknesses.

Next examine the questions that have the largest and smallest standard deviations. A standard deviation is a tool for measuring how much general disagreement or agreement there is around a given question. Those with the smallest deviations are the areas in which there is the greatest degree of agreement in the organization. Those questions with the largest deviations center on the topics of the most disagreement among employees.

Such questions may be provocative areas for further analyses to determine which groups feel positively about the question and which feel negatively. Questions with high deviations suggest issues that may prove to be difficult to resolve quickly within the organization as compared to areas of high agreement. The best approach, when using the data, is to avoid tackling these issues with high standard deviations first. Start change efforts where there is high agreement.

It is important to identify the areas of the highest scores as strength dimensions for the organization. Successful change comes from organizations that recognize strengths and build upon such foundations to address areas of weaknesses. The best pattern for successful organizational change is to recognize strengths and then start with small steps that can yield positive results. As experience comes from successful change, the organization becomes more capable in tackling the more difficult issues.

Analyze the Response Rate

The response rate is the number of surveys completed and returned divided by the number of surveys distributed to employees. It is a first indicator of the level of candor, commitment, and vigor in the organization. Low response levels suggest that the organization has high levels of alienation, indifference, or suspicion. Building trust and reducing defensive, compliant behavior is the first order of business for organizations with low response rates. Response rates that are decreasing from previous levels of survey administrations suggest growing problems of defensive, compliant behavior, indifference, or alienation. Response rates are likely to decline over time when employees do not observe any positive organizational changes resulting from previous surveys.

Be watchful of individual questions that have markedly lower numbers of responses. These may be questions not relevant to some employee groups. They may also represent areas of controversy and defensiveness. Employee unwillingness to respond may be a critical indicator of highly contentious issues, and such areas may be marked for longer-term activities to secure improvement.

Whatever the level of the response, the first critical challenge for the organization is to get the data back to all employees. The danger now is not what the data say about the organization. It is doing nothing or putting the data into a deep freeze. Employees quickly interpret this as meaning that the findings are "bad news" and are likely to become cynical and suspicious. To repeat, the greatest danger in using surveys is doing nothing with the data. In employees' minds, this lack of action calls into question the integrity of the organization's leadership.

1. *Those Who Respond.* The persons who do respond likely represent three groups within the organization: those who respond with the assumption that their answers are simply important to improving organizational functioning; those who are the current cheerleaders and want to make the organization look good; those who are upset with aspects of the current organization and will use the opportunity to identify areas of irritation.

2. *Those Who Do Not Respond.* While some persons will fail to respond because a survey is misplaced, most who do not respond are likely alienated and unwilling to support efforts to promote needed changes. The larger the number not responding, the greater the likelihood that human resources are not fully available for organizational improvement. Rather than being a resource, these persons act as a drag on work to improve and innovate. For example, an organization with a 33 percent response rate is like a six-cylinder engine running on only two cylinders. The response rate is the first tip-off of how well human resources in the organization are deployed.

Validate the Data with Employees

Once organizational survey data are received, the next step—and single most critical one—is closing the loop back to the employees. Data results must be returned to employees immediately to establish ownership and responsibility for the data in order to begin improvements.

The SOE data are too voluminous to simply duplicate and distribute. The most successful approach is to use a progressive tack over a couple of months to roll the findings back to the employees. Small organizations with perhaps fewer than fifty employees might choose to return the data through handouts at a couple of organization-wide meetings. Our experience is that for almost any organization the following procedures work well to get the SOE data back and use the information to "kick start" change.

First, a couple of simple steps can be profitably taken. One is to publish the information in an organizational newsletter with accompanying explanatory text. Usually the data are spread over two or three newsletters. Follow each newsletter with small workgroup discussions and review sessions that provide every organizational member an opportunity to see the findings, discuss their meanings, and offer suggestions for improvement. The discussion meetings promote a sense of accomplishment through a recognition of organizational strengths.

These meetings effectively serve to validate the data with the employees. It fulfills an implied promise when survey participation is requested. The findings are brought back home and the process of using data to promote improvement is begun.

Steps for Validating the Data

Publishing the SOE findings and holding meetings among all employees are critical steps to using the data for change. Here is a suggested and expanded protocol for getting the data back to the employees and using that process to continue the momentum to build a more effective organization.

1. *Review data with executive staff.* Successful change must typically be endorsed by and led from the top of the organization. Data must first be reviewed with the top staff and consensus developed on how to proceed. The best practice is to follow a similar procedure then with all employees. At a minimum, take these three steps:
• Go through the data runs entitled the "20 Constructs and Mean Scores for All Questions." Focus on the two highest and two lowest constructs.
• Look at the specific questions that produce the constructs. Be certain that leadership understands all the strengths and weaknesses as identified by the SOE.
• Develop plans for circulating all data sequentially for all staff.

As the SOE data are reviewed with executive staff, some specific forms are helpful to frame actions. The following forms can be reproduced and used by staff to facilitate returning the SOE data to the organization and developing the change strategies from the data (see Appendix C).
  a. Establishing the Overall Plan with Executive Staff
  b. Assess the Response Rate
  c. Identify the Most Salient Strengths and Weaknesses and Benchmark Them
  d. Designate the Change Team
  e. Work Unit Groups
  f. Report on Top-Priority Change Topic
2. *Spread effort across several meetings.* This is usually done with three or four weekly or monthly reports or organization newsletters that take a portion of the constructs and questions and provide the data along with illustrations pertinent to the given organization. For example if the construct score on Adequacy of Physical Environment is

among the lowest and there is dissatisfaction with computer resources, then move directly to address this issue. Make certain that employees know that this is a concern. Then emphasize that the organization will take steps to address what options exist. Areas such as computer resources or pay levels are good examples of areas that an organization may not be able to change, but it is important to acknowledge these as a problem if they exist. Typically, discussion among employees will move to related topics where change can be achieved.

Be certain to balance areas of needed attention with areas that have high employee ratings. Do not make these meetings simply an opportunity to gripe. High ratings on constructs and individual questions reflect the organization's strengths. Discussion should be balanced on recognizing strengths and addressing weaknesses as opportunities for improvement.

3. *Build the Change Team.* Leadership must build a structure to continue the movement toward positive change. In effect, a long-term Change Team must be put in place to guide and continually spur the movement toward an organization characterized not by control, but by responsibility and innovation. The Change Team needs to be created by the head of the organization and must be in place before publishing the SOE findings.

The Change Team should be composed of a diagonal slice from the organization, representing various organizational functions horizontally as well as including all levels of the organization vertically— from the top to the bottom. In many ways, the organization must build "crosswalks among the silos." Part of the legacy of industrial assembly management has been the creation of highly specialized units that have often tenuous links to other units. In effect, many modern complex bureaucracies consist of impregnable vertical structures, like grain silos. In the silos people go about their business, often quite independent of the broader organizational purpose. In such silos we find the development of jobs that become entitlements, existing for the convenience of the position holder rather than serving the greater whole. Using diagonal slices brings the larger purpose to the independent silos.

The purpose of the Change Team is to coordinate employee feedback and oversee resulting change activities. The Change Team is led by a member of executive management and usually by a person from human resources as well. Several more members are selected from across the organization; the total number of members on the team is approximately eight. In large organizations additional change teams will be necessary in large departments or other large functional units.

It is important to the have executive staff designate the Change Team leader. It is imperative that the Change Team has the full endorsement of the leadership of the organization.

4. *Compare results with benchmark scores and previous survey data.* Positive change rarely comes without data that challenge thinking and suggest better ways of doing things. Various comparison scores or *benchmarks* are available through the SOE to provide a broader context in which to examine each individual organization's data. These are three steps for comparing organizational data.

· Compare your organization's results to what other organizations report and what your data were if available from previous years.

· Locate areas of relative strength and weakness as compared to statewide data.

· If previous administration data are available, see if changes, negative and positive, have occurred.

5. *Roll data back to workgroups so that all staff can discuss the data.* A thinking organization is an organization where there is a high degree of participation in the organization in determining goals and methods in solving problems. It is also an organization where members exercise high levels of personal responsibility for organizational responsibilities. To get the best results in terms of total organizational commitment to change and improvement, everyone needs to take responsibility for the results that come from the data and for developing improvements. In our experience this process works well when it involves all employees in structured workgroups that tackle the data. These are the steps in getting the data back to all of the organization.

· Select a time (the end of the week usually works best) when every employee can participate in a workgroup to review the reports as they are distributed to all staff.

· Restrict the size of the groups to no more than a dozen people at a time and set a specific length of time for the meeting. One to two hours is a sufficient period. Anything beyond two hours is likely to be counterproductive.

· Build the workgroups around actual work units in the organization. Start each meeting by reviewing strengths as indicated in the data report and then brainstorming on how best to address weaknesses.

· If needed, use facilitators to keep the discussion balanced between strengths and weaknesses and to focus activities on how to improve. The responsibility of the groups is to generate ideas for improvement.

· The workgroup leader should make certain that the emphasis is on positive steps to improve, not an exercise in assigning blame! Whining, complaining, or indifference must be dealt with to get the responsibility fully shared by all.

· Have each group report back by selecting one or two essential areas and proposing a Six-Month Plan to address the areas.

· Take all the proposed plans to the Change Team. That team then prepares the first set of improvement efforts.

· Take the work of the Change Team to the executive staff and get their sign-off.

· The Change Team then directs a coordinated program to undertake the change throughout the organization. This activity, in collaboration with and through each work unit, will provide specific steps to implement the Six-Month Plan.

· After the first activities, select a second couple of important areas and repeat the process.

6. *Set six-month time horizons.* One might ask how long this change process should continue and why six-month time horizons should be set. The answer is that the change process must be continuous. In turbulent times an organization must continually assess its goals and methods and relate those to challenges and opportunities. There is nothing in our external environment to suggest any immediate change to less turbulent times.

The six-month horizon is a simple rule of thumb. It is long enough to get many processes underway and see some results. Some processes are amenable to shorter time periods and others will change only over many more months. The six-month rule is to get people focused on a specific activity and into the habit of making change, sticking with it, and measuring for results. These suggested procedures for using the data with employees' help create a self-sustaining pattern within the culture of the organization. With this pattern or cultural norm, everyone becomes involved in continuous quality improvement.

7. *Re-measure for results.* After a change activity is completed, then it is time to re-measure to see if the intended results did occur. Part of ensuring that continuous change becomes integrated within the organization, instead of an occasional effort, requires that all routine employee evaluation measures include material on how change efforts are created and addressed. Supervisory evaluation especially must contain reference to active and continuous leadership in change activities.

Choosing the Path and Goals

As survey data are distributed and discussed, the strategy of change, supported with goals and procedures, starts to materialize. Part of the discussion phase with small groups is to create the necessary ownership and empowerment to get each employee involved in devising changes and taking responsibility for participating in the desired changes.

Take Small, Concrete Steps First

It is very important to start the change activity off with small, discrete steps. For an organization to develop a sense of competency in analyzing itself and learning a strong sense of critique with a focus on making positive changes, experience must come from success.

Start Where Success Can Come Quickly

The idea of selecting activities that permit ready accomplishment in order to get some success under the belt helps to build both momentum and the necessary commitment to take risks to improve. Always start with activities that have clear, concrete, and relatively rapid returns.

As progress begins, then a larger process can evolve for specifying the vision of where the organization plans to be in the distance, such as two or three years hence.

The Traditional Paradigm

Under the traditional management control paradigm, employees occupy roles largely similar to machines on the shop floor. They are positioned on a long assembly line, perform activities designated by the structure of the organization, and are controlled by a supervisor. The personal perspectives and concerns of employees are often viewed as illegitimate. Moreover, such concerns may be seen as threats to the rational order of the organization. To the extent that the voices of employees are heard, they often come through external organizations, such as unions, which may pose challenges to the authority of traditional bureaucratic organizations.

Successful change is in many instances movement away from the traditional paradigm to a model of the organization that permits quick adaptation and innovation. Such a model requires very different relations with the members of the organization, and change must include working with employees to recast these relations.

Focus on Empowerment

Empowerment is a mobilizing force for the modern thinking organization. It is the single most important energy source to tap to begin the process of creating a new and far more vital organization. To maintain innovation and rapid rates of change in the face of highly competitive and turbulent environments, successful organizations cannot exist as machines that produce, on a mass scale, large quantities of similar products or services. Rather, organizations must exist as decentralized entities that shape product and services continuously to meet changing customer demands and environmental opportunities. Instead of being controlled by management, these employees are inspired by leadership and intimately involved in designing and creating products and services. Empowerment is employees feeling highly invested in what they do, close to those who use the product or service, and willing to improve and lead. Empowerment is employees being responsible, focused on goals, and ready to respond to change and challenges.

Bumps in the Road

Successful change is never completely smooth sailing with sunny days and favorable winds. Challenges abound, and here are some of the more significant bumps along the road in dealing with people in the organization.

Dealing with the World-Weary

One of the more debilitating forces that thwarts change is the organizational sophisticate who affects a stance like that of the world-weary expatriates of old movies, such as Humphrey Bogart in *Casablanca*. As the proprietor of Rick's American Bar, he has seen the world in all its venality and pettiness and seeks to be indifferent to it. Like their counterparts of two generations ago in Europe or North Africa, the world-weary of today feel that they have seen it all and have enthusiasm only for dismissing ideals of excellence, striving, and dedication. When change is proposed and the call for heroism is issued, their motto is "been there, done that" or "this too will pass."

Dealing with Bureaucracy Builders

A second debilitating personality is the kind of individual who has been most successful in the old bureaucratic paradigm. These are persons skilled in building organizations, co-opting the work of the innovators, soothing anxieties, giving orders, and presiding over yet stifling competition and innovation. Often they take a simple process and create needless steps, checkpoints, and positions subordinate to them. The bureaucracy builders thrive by taking the work of others and laying claim to it while doing none themselves. Their special genius is to position themselves at the head of a parade and take credit for any accomplishment.

Dealing with Snakes

Regrettably in most organizations there are persons who are best described simply as *snakes*.[6] These individuals succeed by pitting persons against each other and maintaining gossip lines and rumor mills that induce uneasiness and distrust. Snakes lie in the tall grass and maintain their positions by promoting fear and anxiety among others. Snakes engender uncertainty and create an atmosphere inimical to trust and risk taking. Like the bureaucracy builders, they are creatures of the old paradigm, and thus destructive entities in the new paradigm of leadership and participative empowerment.

Mistakes in Seeking Change

Finally, here are a few mistakes to be avoided when seeking successful change:
- Making participation a volunteer effort
- Appointing a quality coordinator with little or no power
- Waiting to survey until things quiet down
- Waiting to survey until people feel better
- Dealing with quality as a "flavor of the month" activity
- Using a reengineering/reorganizing approach from the top down —the "chainsaw" approach to change
- Depending upon outside consultants to define and lead the effort
- Failing to get the support of top leadership
- Failing to make continuous change a permanent part of how work is done

Visionary leadership must recognize these throwbacks to the old paradigm and ensure that trust, commitment, and empowerment do not become derailed by notions no longer relevant to the modern organizations. Involving employees in using data to improve is the first step in recognizing the imperative for change and moving toward a paradigm of leadership, not bureaucratic control and stagnation.

One More Time

The SOE is not an end to itself, but an assist in creating organizations that are responsive to both customers and the larger community and provide meaning, support, and fulfillment to the members of the organization. The data are an important tool for leadership to change the properties of an organization so that it reacts quickly, innovates when needed, responds to the environment, and makes people feel fulfilled and productive.

The first step is to roll the data back to the employees to get their "buy in" and acceptance of responsibility. Use the organizational data to generate comparisons with other related information (benchmarks) such as statewide scores. Examine the strengths and weaknesses and take credit for the strengths. Find some small steps to take that will build confidence and willingness to take on larger changes. Make a plan that will last for several months.

Changing an organization is more like growing a tree than painting a picture. Progress occurs over the months, and large-scale organizational and cultural change will take several years. So prepare landmarks along the way and keep a record of accomplishments to maintain the sense of progress and pursuit toward goals. Remember to use the SOE data with all employees and work to create a norm of searching for improvements as a regular part of work. Efforts to improve organizations and increase quality fail when they are handled just by a few or when they occur only occasionally.

A thinking organization comes into being because all employees learn to fully participate and search for ways to improve. Our experience indicates an essential concept. Everyone *participates* and *searches endlessly for improvements!* This is a defining characteristic for the entire organization.

Remember to maintain a sense of urgency throughout the organization. Create zeal for improvement and the discovery of better ways. Organizations, like people, do not stand still. Success comes only with the continual pursuit of improvement, of perfection, of excellence!

Summary

The first five chapters have presented in concrete detail what the Survey of Organizational Excellence is, why and how one uses the survey, and how the data are summarized to help set an agenda for specific and continuous organizational improvement. Three things make up outstanding, successful organizations:

1. Vigorous and *visionary* leadership that can inspire trust, openness, dedication, and striving in employees
2. *Internal data* that provide all employees a forum around which to understand the organization and its process
3. *External data* that provide information about the way clients, customers, regulators, and competitors perceive the organization

This chapter offers a model of how leadership can take the SOE data and organizational assessment back to the employees of the organization and use these data to build stronger, more creative and capable organizations. Chapter 6 provides some representative information of the findings of the survey and how the information is used by organizations to address problems and increase quality.

6 | Some Results from Organizations Using the SOE

Just after the close of the Texas legislative session in June 1997, I met with a senior official of the Legislative Budget Board, John Barton. John has been among a group of Texas officials and legislators that have led efforts to focus state activities on specific problems. Improved budgeting procedures, measures of effectiveness, steps to measure service quality, and clearly focused goals for state organizations have come from these leadership efforts.[1] With the state's population growing rapidly, these activities are critical to providing the right services matched to the right needs. John observed with some sense of pride that Texas now has arguably the most thorough strategic planning process of any state. Knowing how critical state services in health, safety, transportation, and education are to both the immediate well-being of the state and to the future, he and his agency, the Legislative Budget Board, have long been advocates for sound planning. This body has urged agencies to set their goals clearly and to find ways continuously to improve programs and accomplishments. Yet in the next breath, he tempered his observations by noting that, to date, "We are still trying to figure out how to use strategic planning (and performance budgeting) to improve education and health, reduce crime, and generally address effectively those needs that are the responsibility of state government. Until we see more results we do not know if we can improve government as we hope."

This chapter provides information on general patterns of strengths and weaknesses in the participating agencies and some concrete data on actual changes that are underway in agencies. Even these data, though, are still one step removed from the information that John Barton cited as essential to the proof of strategic planning. However, they provide distinct examples of the ways in which agencies are using the SOE data to make organizational improvements.

With the development of the SOE in 1993, groundwork was completed for a variety of short- and long-term examinations of the findings both within and among organizations.

Excellence Comes from the Opportunity to Compare

It is very difficult for genuine improvement to occur in an organization without convenient means to compare what an organization does against the work of other organizations. In the classic sense of production and trading, the existence of a market in the private sector serves that function of continuous comparison. If one is shopping for fresh fish, vegetables, and fruits, a market with several competitors will serve to promote the highest quality and the lowest prices. The shop whose produce is stale, lacking in taste, or overpriced must either meet the competition or go out of existence. Shops will compete to be the first to have the new season's strawberries or the freshest catch of oysters or sea bass. Word travels quickly among customers, and businesses must be nimble to continue to meet the competition. This is how markets serve to identify superior products and services and create prices matched to outputs.[2]

However, more complex products such as automobiles, housing, appliances, and consumer electronics present greater challenges in determining quality. An automobile that is pleasant to drive for the first ten thousand miles may prove to be an unreliable headache later. The carpeting that looks so attractive when new may soil or mat readily and require replacement too soon. To supplement the market and make the purchaser more knowledgeable about such goods, different kinds of ratings services have developed in modern economies. Whole publishing industries exist that test, price, and compare such products and provide the consumer with a valuable addition to market forces.[3]

Services have proven more elusive to evaluate. Some services such as housekeeping, laundry and dry cleaning, restaurants, and hair cutting lend themselves readily to comparisons, and word of mouth serves as a market function. Other services such as medical care, legal services, and professional training or higher education are difficult to compare in terms of quality. In many cases, it is not that the service is so complex or abstruse, but that adequate data are not available to permit comparisons. Such services are *intangible*. They are not readily tasted, felt, or seen. Though not inconsequential, the process of comparison and ready evaluation has been slippery.

For a manufacturer, the product itself is an important data element for improving quality. The product can be carefully examined by others and compared with other similar products. Services may be less visible and difficult to compare with another similar service even if one exists. For example, when one uses the services of a physician or attorney, it is more difficult to determine the quality than it is to judge the freshness and price of flounder or tuna at the market. Moreover, unlike automobiles or television sets, there are no magazine or ratings services that provide data on quality, price, durability, service warranties, and so forth. In a similar fashion when the high school senior has to choose among the local community college, the state university, and the private institution, clear and useful comparative market data upon which to base decisions are difficult to find. In all these cases, recommendations of friends and general reputation are about the extent of the market data available.[4] As a means to ensure quality, the professions and higher education have developed various self-regulating bodies or boards. Medical and legal groups have licensing standards that determine who is eligible to apply for practice, examining groups, and local, state, and national standard-setting associations. Institutions of higher education have regional and national certifying associations that regularly review programs and entire institutions and make recommendations to assure quality.

Yet these professional, self-regulating approaches are far less adequate than general markets where genuine competition exists. The data they accumulate on things such as the standards of practice of an attorney or the conduct of a physician during a surgery are rarely available to the public and, thus, the consumer. Similarly, the accrediting bodies of colleges, hospitals, and clinics rarely publish their findings and rankings of entities that are reviewed. Indeed, it may be argued that such "closed systems" of review do not serve to promote quality but rather to restrict competition and lessen innovation.

Government services, which are often monopolistic, are even more susceptible to such problems of no competition, little meaningful review, and restricted public access to information about services. For these service entities, steps must be taken to create the appropriate data sets to describe the service and set the means in motion for improving quality. Without market feedback, organizations such as government must be especially sensitive and thoughtful about the definition of quality in services rendered. Without competition and the ready comparisons that true markets provide, the goals of quality, innovation, and lower costs demand greater dedication to achieving such goals.

Two conclusions are inescapable when examining where improvements in quality occur, where rates of innovation are high, and where there are efforts to reduce the cost of the service or product. One is that there must be clear, readily accessible data about the service or product. To have markets with fresher, crisper apples or more comfortable and dependable cars, there must be data about the products. The second conclusion is that there must be markets, means of making comparisons among the products or services. If there is only one shop that sells apples or only one brand of automobile, there is little room for comparison, much less alternatives.

Creating Benchmarks for the Intangibles

One of the distinctive values of the SOE is that the findings serve both of these conclusions. The SOE is designed to provide clear, readily accessible data about how organizations function and on dimensions that are often thought to be intangible. Since comparable dimensions are measured on all organizations, then ready comparisons can be made with other organizations. The SOE data accessible through the database of participating organizations provide an inventory of benchmarks and best practices. The fact that these data exist and are available to agencies, the Governor's Office, and the Legislature set important expectations that data are being gathered and improvement is expected. Indeed one of the more striking findings of the use of the SOE is the extent to which state executives now expect these data and grow concerned about organizations that do not collect data.

General Findings across Organizations

The revised SOE has been in place for four years. Extensive information is now available that describes the kinds of organizations that are using the SOE and the ways it is used.

Rising Response Rates

One of the clearest indicators of improvement in organizations is the sharp increase in employee participation in the SOE that was recorded between 1994 and 1996. The average response rate per agency increased from 42 percent in 1994 to 60 percent in 1996. This significant increase in participation clearly indicates the presence of a state workforce where both agency leaders and rank-and-file state employees are increasingly concerned about the need to improve organizational performance and work life. Additionally, participants seem to be viewing the SOE as a credible means of putting their thoughts and evaluations before organizational and state leadership. But this is a two-edged sword. Employees are eager for greater participation and responsibility, but corresponding moves must be made from leadership.

The detailed response characteristics for the last two SOE administrations indicate that the SOE data are representative of the Texas state workforce. One important achievement for the state is that the two largest ethnic minorities in Texas are close to being proportionally represented within the state workforce. This is vital for two reasons. One is that state organizations must be representative of the general population to maintain the loyalty and support of citizens. Representative government does mean that government organizations must be perceived by the people as representative of the people. The second reason is that most of government is providing services, not producing goods. Part of providing effective services is having employees that are sensitive to, empathetic with customers and clients. To the degree that employees and customers share similar cultural characteristics, the likelihood of such sensitivity is increased.

This proportionality within the state workforce does not extend to all levels of the organization, though, and minorities are relatively underrepresented in higher-paying positions and those that require higher levels of education and training. Moreover, minority groups participate in the SOE at a lower rate than the majority ethnic group, although rates for minority groups increased from 1994–1995 to 1996–1997. This would suggest increased feelings of involvement, responsibility, and empowerment among minority group employees and is one dimension that should be closely watched in each SOE administration. Table 1 presents general demographic information for Texas state organization participants.

Table 1. Demographic Profile of SOE Respondents

	State Workforce [1] (%)	1996–1997 Respondents [2] (%)	1994–1995 Respondents [3] (%)
Gender			
Male	47.40	41.35	47.32
Female	52.60	57.05	50.76
Missing		01.60	01.92
Race/Ethnicity			
African-American	17.60	09.32	06.78
Hispanic-American	20.36	18.33	16.33
Anglo-American	60.50	64.72	68.74
Asian-American, Native American, or Pacific Islander	01.53	01.83	01.71
Other	00.02	02.78	03.05
Missing		03.02	03.39

[1] Texas government workforce data as reported to USPS/HRIS as of June 30, 1996; data exclude institutions of higher education.
[2] Surveys distributed to 72,203 state employees; 30,318 valid responses returned.
[3] Surveys distributed to 60,189 state employees; 17,925 valid responses returned.

Continuing Focus on Customer Service

Customer service issues continue to receive high-priority attention in state organizations. Relative to other areas addressed in the SOE, aspects of customer service such as the organization's communications with constituents and the quality of services provided to customers are viewed by state employees as areas that continue to improve. For several years, state and agency leadership and state training resources have emphasized the need to improve the quality of state services. The SOE data support the positive impact that these activities are having on employee perceptions of their organizations' services. Routinely across all agencies and for statewide averages, the questions that address the perceived quality of the services provided have the highest rankings.

Increasing Dissatisfaction with the Compensation Package

Survey results emphasize that state employees are less satisfied with their overall compensation package than they were two years ago. Dissatisfaction is growing, especially in the area of wage compensation. Employees are generally more positive when asked specifically about the employment benefits package. These findings suggest that the overall compensation package receives mixed reviews among state employees; nevertheless, the data clearly indicate that employees perceive the overall competitiveness of the package as declining during the last two years.

Such data indicate one of the larger leadership challenges faced by the state agencies described in this book. Organizational improvement and the creation of higher-quality services do not readily translate into increased revenues for the organization. They may indeed for a manufacturer or a business that provides services such as a restaurant or a hospital. In state government, though, revenues are largely generated through taxation that is somewhat independent of each agency's service activities. Even in those state agencies that generate all of their budgets through fees, fines, and licenses, the budget for the organization is set by the state legislature. Moreover, the budget-setting process still uses "across the board" strategies, and the outstanding progress by one agency may be drowned by poorer quality elsewhere in other agencies. Legislators may also not perceive quality differences or feel that increases in quality are worth additional dollars. Service organizations, particularly those of government, often face the challenge of both increasing quality and then making certain that consumers recognize the increase.

Raises and Promotions Not Connected to Work Performance

The question that received the lowest score for the 1996–1997 SOE was the following: "Raises and promotions are designed to ensure that workers are rewarded solely for their performance." With approximately 70 percent of employees either disagreeing or strongly disagreeing with this statement, it is clear that state employees do not see a link between the quality of an individual's work performance and resulting raise and promotion opportunities. Such data suggest the following employee perceptions:

- The continuation of "old boy" and "old girl" networks that control advancement
- The lack of equal opportunity for employees based upon work performance
- An organizational culture that does not value excellence

This finding and similar data from questions that deal with the quality of supervision and the support for innovation imply that respondents feel strongly that critical policies affecting individual perceptions of fairness and appropriate work expectations are askew. Indeed what many organizations are facing is a workforce that wants to improve and innovate and yet feels that supervisory leadership does not match these intentions. If organizations are to continue to achieve progress in improving the quality of services, employees must feel that advancement is based upon factors associated with job performance. It seems critically important in the coming years for the organizations to invest deeply in either making their supervisory process more focused on performance or making certain that employees see that support for improvement does exist.

Improved Computer Resources and Information Sharing

While the 1994–1995 SOE found many agencies lacking in information resources, the most recent survey suggests that substantial improvements have been made. The 1996–1997 SOE results show improvement in employee access to needed computer (hardware and software) resources. Perhaps consistent with this finding, employees also report improvements in inter- and intra-agency information sharing. Survey results indicate improvement in agencies' infrastructures, improvements that will help Texas move into the information age. These advancements indicate that state organizations are becoming much more efficient and up to date in performing a basic function of government: processing of information.

Expanding Opportunities for Working Alternative Schedules

Survey results suggest that opportunities for state employees to work nontraditional schedules have increased during the last two years. In the 1996–1997 administration, 58 percent of all respondents agreed or strongly agreed with the survey question "Alternative work schedules (flex-time, compressed work weeks, job sharing) are offered to employees." In 1994–1995 47 percent of respondents responded favorably. With 60 percent of all respondents reporting that there is more than one wage earner in their household, opportunities for working schedules other than 8 to 5 likely assist employees in meeting personal, family, and community obligations.

While these expanded opportunities have undeniable benefits for employees, they also provide less visible but vital benefits to the community. Flexible time means employees have more time to deal with responsibilities such as attending teacher conferences at school, taking children to medical appointments, school, and community events, participating in church and community activities, and so on.

Organizational Culture Limits Innovation and Participation

The overall assessment of the culture that exists in many state organizations is one of the most troubling findings in the SOE data, which paint a picture of an organizational culture in which the status quo is valued by organization leadership. Creativity, innovation, and individual employee initiatives are not perceived as being encouraged; employees are offered few opportunities to participate in long-term planning, and there is a lack of trust between employees and management. Creativity, innovation, trust, and ownership of work are all critical components of a work environment that can successfully meet both customer and employee expectations. The SOE data suggest that state agencies are making few gains in these areas.

Using Intervention Categories (Dimensions) as Benchmarks

Survey data readily permit benchmarking between organizations and comparisons to statewide averages. Table 2 presents data from three state organizations using the five dimensions detailed in Chapter 4 (Work Team, Work Settings/Accommodations, General Organizational Features, Communication Patterns, and Personal Demands). By arraying these scores in a table and creating an additional average for the five dimensions called Synthesis, we have a good thumbnail sketch of three separate organizations. As the data show, Agency A is facing substantial challenge in all areas. Agency B, while having scores barely on the positive side of these dimensions, shows clear areas of strength. Agency C has quite high scores and is an entity that serves as a high-level benchmark for other agencies.

Each of these three organizations may use these data and comparisons differently. Agency C has the challenge of maintaining its strong position while targeting some specific area to build improvements. The

Table 2. A Comparison of Construct Scores for Three Agencies

Agency	Dimension I Work Team	Dimension II Work Settings/ Accommo- dations	Dimension III General Organiza- tional Features	Dimension IV Communi- cation Patterns	Dimension V Personal Demands	Synthesis
A	226	263	249	227	239	241
B	325	342	358	322	338	337
C	412	404	437	423	400	415
Statewide	301	331	334	320	312	320
Minimum	100	100	100	100	100	100
Maximum	500	500	500	500	500	500

Personal Dimension is the lowest; one way to start would be to look at specific constructs or individual questions to locate areas that demand attention. Agency B may find it useful to look first at the Communication Patterns and Work Team dimensions. Agency A will probably benefit most from tackling all dimensions from the outset. While its scores are low, the fact that it used the SOE and now has the data is a significant strength. This is already an indicator that the organization is seeking improvement. Organizations improve only when they start to look at themselves and gather data to promote improvement. Agency A has plenty to work on; yet the prognosis is favorable since the most difficult step—gathering information—has begun.

Statewide Recommendations Comparing 1994–1995 and 1996–1997 Surveys

The SOE permits conclusions to be drawn about a large universe of organizations. From the State of Texas survey data for two different years, five important recommendations can be made.

1. *Agencies should continue to stress their efforts in improving customer service orientation.* Solid progress has been made, but citizens'

expectations remain high and call for more increases in quality, responsiveness, and availability. Findings that came from the Texas Poll in August 1996 support the need to continue the emphasis on improving quality.[5] Those data indicated that Texans are generally pleased with the quality of services provided by state government and can see positive changes during the last two years. However, the same data suggest that citizens have even higher expectations of where quality levels should be. Moreover, they are less convinced of the need for salary increases than are state employees. The focus on quality demands continuous attention at all levels of the organization and in all state agencies. SOE data provide a ready mechanism for each organization to initiate long-term improvement projects to increase service quality.

2. *Agency leadership should increase the emphasis on supervisory procedures and training to tie raises and promotions to work performance.* How decisions are made pertaining to raises and promotions needs to be more clearly articulated to all employees. Concerns about the quality of supervision and the low level of trust in the workplace that employees report are areas that need far greater attention. The sharp increases in almost every agency in the rate of employee participation in the SOE is a strong, positive vote cast by employees in the belief that their organizations seek to enhance organizational quality. To support this belief, focused attention needs to be directed toward improving supervision, tying performance clearly to employee evaluation, and effectively communicating such procedures to every employee. For organizations to be innovative and efficient, there must be highly capable leadership and supervision as well as high levels of trust and commitment from employees to the organization. Much work lies ahead in this area for state organizations.

3. *Some measure should be enacted to address inequities in compensation for some or all employees.* Employees feel strongly that compensation levels do not match those provided by other levels of government and private employers. With meager compensation increases over several years, coupled with rising living costs, employees are especially concerned about salary levels. Moreover, certain jobs and locations are more adversely affected by pay inadequacies, and it may be time to identify certain positions and locations that qualify for variances in the uniform wage system to attract and retain employees.

4. *Efforts should be continued to promote changes in work schedules that permit individuals to vary schedules from an eight-hour day and*

five-day work week. Such changes do not add cost to the agency and substantially assist employees in meeting family and community obligations. The fact that in many families both adult wage earners work outside the home complicates childcare responsibilities, schooling duties, and assistance that may be required for aged family members. Advances in communication and computer technology are quickly changing the need for all employees to be at one job site at one time for work to be done. Permitting schedule variation makes good sense for agencies, employees, families, and communities.

5. *State agencies need to be more active in enlisting employees in efforts in long-term planning and goal setting.* Leadership must look for more opportunities to appropriately mobilize employees in examining better ways to get work done and to improve agency responsiveness to the public. Outstanding organizations fully use all resources, and no organization should fail to enlist employees in long-term and large-scale planning and goal setting. Every state agency has thousands of processes and deals with the public in a multitude of ways. When employees participate in planning and goal setting, they bring to bear a rich variety of experiences to suggest improvement and, in turn, see how individual jobs contribute to the total activity of the organization.

Only one of these five recommendations has direct budgetary consequences. Moreover, all five represent not the linear strategy of the past that calls for more resources to deal with change but rather better ways of doing what needs to be done. An important learning that must be gleaned from the winds of change rushing through organizations today is that each person must learn to work smarter. These recommendations, many of which are now underway in several state agencies, are part of the process of inventing better ways. Appendix D provides a list of the organizational participants in the SOE and persons in each organization leading survey activities. Various organizational benchmarks are provided in this appendix, and the SOE Web site provides the most recent updates.

Moving from Internal Data to External Data: Examining Customer Satisfaction

Remember, though, that the SOE data are *internal* data. They measure what organizational members think are strengths and weaknesses. Of equal importance is what the users of services feel about the

Table 3. Comparison of Perceptions of Average Citizens and State Employees

	Texas Poll	Score	Survey of Organizational Excellence	Score
1	Agencies of Texas state government are known for the high quality of their customer service.	3.1	We are known for our customer service.	3.6
2	Texas state agencies serve the public well.	3.3	We work well with the public.	3.8
3	Texas state government is known in your area as an employer that offers competitive salaries.	3.2	Salaries are competitive with similar jobs in the community.	2.3
4	Texas state agencies produce high-quality work with few errors.	2.8	We produce high-quality work that has a low rate of error.	3.6
5	Over the last two years, the quality of services provided by agencies of Texas state government has improved.	3.2	Assess the quality of service that this organization provides to its customers.	3.5

Scoring convention for questions 1–4:
1 = strongly disagree
2 = disagree
3 = feel neutral
4 = agree
5 = strongly agree

Scoring convention for question 5:
1 = the organization is performing much worse than two years ago
2 = the organization is performing worse than two years ago
3 = the organization is the same as it was two years ago
4 = the organization is performing better than two years ago
5 = the organization is performing much better than two years ago

quality dimension. We requested the Texas Poll in August 1996 to ask a sample of Texans how they rated the quality of services provided. The polling results and the comparable data from state employees are discussed below.

Data in Table 3 permit us to compare how employees of state government view their efforts as compared with views of average citizens. The first column of questions are from the Texas Poll and were directed to a randomly chosen 1,001 persons interviewed by telephone. The questions in the second column are worded a bit differently since the Survey of Organizational Excellence is directed toward state employees. The scores are the mean (arithmetic average) values calculated by the scoring convention that is detailed below the table. Scores above 3.0 represent areas that are viewed more positively; scores below 3.0 are areas viewed more negatively.

Key Findings Comparing Citizens with State Employees

Perhaps what is most significant about the Poll results is that although citizen responses were less positive than those of state employees, average Texas Poll respondents still viewed state agencies as responding well to the citizenry of Texas. In addition, approximately 26 percent of the Poll respondents reported that state agencies are performing better than they were two years ago.

Most Poll respondents' greatest concern was the quality of services that are provided by state agencies. When addressing this dimension of state government, Poll respondents had less favorable perceptions than state employees, particularly with respect to errors. This difference is somewhat expected because employees inside an organization performing the work are likely to view it more positively than persons outside the organization. Organizations that deliver high levels of quality have members that are proud of their work, and SOE data indicate that Texas government employees have pride in their accomplishments. Nevertheless, the Texas Poll data indicate that citizens have even higher expectations.

This comparison between employees and citizens will be an important area to continue to observe over the next few years as quality initiatives continue to expand and mature in Texas state agencies. Statewide SOE results from 1994 and 1996 suggest that customer focus and high quality services have received increasing emphasis over the last few years among state agencies. Employees feel that clear improvement has occurred; however, the data indicate that employees believe there is room for continued improvements in their organizations.

The issue of the competitiveness of salaries offered by state government is the area of most disagreement between state employees and respondents of the Texas Poll. Texas Poll respondents were much more likely to perceive that state government offers competitive salaries than were state employees. Survey results from 1994 indicate that state employees residing in urban areas of the state, including Houston, Dallas, and Austin, are the most dissatisfied with salaries. While most persons are likely to feel that they need more compensation, the degree of frustration by state employees on this dimension appears substantial.

Implications

Together the SOE data and the Texas Poll data provide important comparisons or benchmarks about producers and consumers of governmental services. Generally, one can conclude that state government services are viewed as having quality, but both the average citizen and the state employee see room for improvement. Citizens clearly see relatively poorer performance than what employees assess. We must watch these benchmarks closely at future points to see if quality efforts underway increase the perception of quality by citizens and employees alike. One question raised by such data is this: what is the appropriate organization to compare or benchmark against for state agencies? Since many government services are a monopoly, can you make comparisons without competitors? The answer is yes, you must. In reality, citizens have preferences about the various levels of government. For example, one might ask which levels are more trustworthy. We asked the Texas Poll to do that to determine whether citizens do benchmark across levels of government. When asked to compare the services from the federal to the state to the local level, the Poll reported clear differences: 43 percent of those responding said the local level is most trustworthy, 35 percent rated the state level as the most trustworthy, and only 22 percent selected the federal level.

You Must Benchmark against the World

The reality of our world today is that every organization sets standards of quality and competition for every other organization. The competition is anyone who raises customer expectations!

The implications of this statement for all organizations are enormous. This means that if the mail order merchant L. L. Bean answers every call within five minutes, people will expect the same from the Texas Real Estate Commission and every other governmental organization. If Southwest Airlines enables you to use your computer to make plane reservations, then the Texas Department of Public Safety will face expectations of people seeking to renew driver's licenses just as conveniently. Toyota or Ford can now produce an automobile that averages fewer than twenty flaws and runs for 50,000 with minimum maintenance. Such an achievement will come to mean that employers will soon expect high schools to produce seniors who can write and read with very few grammatical errors and make change without mistakes when they work as store clerks. An open world with a free flow of information means a lot of opportunity for benchmarks. It causes a very high rate of competition and a continuous struggle to improve to keep up with the competition. The reality of the Texas Poll data is that each repeated polling will show an increased standard of quality that state agencies must meet.

Why Do Organizations Participate in the Survey?

Not every agency of Texas state government participates in the Survey of Organizational Excellence. Each agency must decide to participate and pay for the service. Those agencies that do participate take some real chances. Employee expectations are raised that the organization will address complaints. The Governor's Office and the Texas Legislature receive the data and can directly discern both strengths and weaknesses. Agency board members have information that can be used to the detriment of agency executives. Additionally, unlike workers in private businesses, employees in state agencies have little or no direct financial incentive to improve quality, innovate, or reduce costs. In the example of the fresh produce market, if the owner does a better job, there will be more customers and more profits. That is simply not the case for state agencies. Budgets may be set with only marginal concern for the quality of services provided by the agency. Leadership may be chosen or retained because of accomplishment or leadership may be selected because of affiliation with the current political leadership.

Agencies that participate do so because leadership recognizes change in the expectations of government is underway. To repeat, there are three elements to the process of organizational excellence, *visionary leadership, internal data,* and *external data.* Visionary leadership uses the SOE as one of several tools, not to maintain the past but to build the agency of the future. The benchmarking process is well underway, and state leadership looks to every state organization to use the organization fully in promoting excellence. Lastly, citizens are applying the same yardsticks to all sectors of the culture and economy. Put simply, better quality in fresher produce or better cars raises expectations for everything.

Illustrations of Efforts Underway in Organizational Improvement

Agencies are putting the SOE data to use in a variety of ways. When the survey was expanded to permit all state agencies to participate, some agencies saw participation as meaning compliance. In some cases, there was no activity in the organization beyond the initial step to see that employees received the survey. Now, though, fewer agencies are participating solely from this traditional compliance viewpoint.

Efforts to Build Thinking Organizations

As organizations take steps to increase employee participation and responsibility, dozens of exciting innovations are underway. Here are a few illustrations of the ways the SOE provides agencies with data and procedures to develop specific goals for organizational change.

Innovations in Flex-Time: Texas Department of Insurance

The Texas Department of Insurance is an illustration of how an agency can use the SOE data to identify strategic points for change and improvement. Much of the work of this regulatory agency involves communication with citizens who have questions about insurance and policy-enforcement issues with insurance companies. Several major problems that its employees felt they faced were how to meet various family and community obligations: childcare, school and church activities, and household management. The agency began to examine how it could vary working hours to provide employees more alternatives in terms of free time. Morris Wynn and Ann Cook, who led the effort, began to work with the various division managers in the organization. They soon found that there were clear advantages to work patterns other than a five-days-a-week, eight-hours-a-day routine. Working closely with supervisors Wynn and Cook created a variety of different schedules for employees. These alternatives maximized opportunities for employees to meet family and community responsibilities while increasing the organization's ability to respond to the needs of its constituencies. Indeed TDI has become a major source of technical assistance to other organizations seeking to develop flex-time policies.

TDI began a comprehensive business planning process last year as a part of a larger Partnership for Excellence project. TDI joined with agency employees, insurance industry groups, and consumers to develop a road map for achieving the agency's long-term strategic goals.

SOE data are openly shared with each program manager. They are being used by the agency's training department to assist in the design, delivery, and evaluation of a continuously improving training program, especially in the areas of cultural diversity and valuing differences. As the business planning process continues, TDI will use future survey results to monitor improvements in agency morale as well as to provide a communication tool between rank-and-file employees and management. The SOE also provides a means to benchmark successful programs in other agencies.

Employee-Organization Partnerships: Texas Department of Health

With a workforce that exceeds 6,000 employees located throughout the entire state, the Texas Department of Health faces the challenge of finding a way to use SOE findings to positively affect every employee, but in a manner that is cost-efficient. TDH has taken a decentralized approach to working with SOE results. Results have been incorporated into some of the agency's routine training activities; data are used during training sessions where employees from every level of the organization are present. Currently, SOE findings are also being incorporated into the strategic planning process of the Human Resources and Development division, as well as elements of the agency's total quality initiative. All of TDH's survey-related activities have emphasized openness about agency problems and shared responsibility among employees and management for agency improvement.

Most recently, the TDH Learning Council, using a process lasting several months, has begun distributing statewide, agency, and divisional data to every employee in the organization. Each employee will examine statewide and department-wide data as benchmarks against the data for his or her division. Employees will then identify division and agency goals for excellence as well as individual goals. TDH efforts provide an especially clear and focused example of fostering empowerment and accountability among employees at all levels in moving to greater excellence.

Using the SOE with Quality Initiatives: Texas Commission on Fire Protection

Created in 1991, the Texas Commission on Fire Protection is one of Texas' newer state agencies. SOE data were used to complement TCFP's Texas Quality Service initiative, a program that promotes continuous improvement principles, such as customer service and employee participation within the agency. Believing that surveys do little for improvement unless the results are shared openly within the organization, TCFP released all results in the employee newsletter over a two-month period. The agency then provided concurrent opportunities for employees to "feedback" their concerns about the SOE findings to the executive staff. The SOE served as an instrument to facilitate open discussions, and it has directly led to the development of three employee quality teams.

The SOE as a Transition Tool to a New Culture: Texas Employment Commission/Texas Workforce Commission

When the SOE was distributed to state employees in the fall of 1994, the employees of the Texas Employment Commission were not aware that the agency would begin a transition into becoming the Texas Workforce Commission. TEC staff expects that the 1994 SOE data will provide a benchmark for the agency to utilize in the years to come. TEC regional managers and department heads have analyzed SOE data in order to implement improvement activities at the local level. In addition, TEC's Human Resource personnel are analyzing SOE results specific to their division and developing a model that may be replicated by other divisions in the organization.

Moving from the Third World of State Agencies: Texas Real Estate Commission

One of the more straightforward uses of the SOE, starting from the 1994 administration, was a set of activities by the Texas Real Estate Commission. This agency, with approximately 70 employees, is one of the many small agencies in state government. It has the responsibility of licensing realtors and regulating certain aspects of the real estate industry, including areas such as apartment rentals and time-share condominiums. The agency serves both real estate professionals and members of the public that rent and purchase housing and land. Much of its business is done via phone calls coming into the state offices, training programs that it delivers, and licensing processes of realtors. Thus a phone call may be from someone highly trained in the real estate business or from a worried purchaser of a condominium who needs help in knowing what rights he or she may have.

As a regulatory agency, the Commission raises considerably more funds than it uses in the operation of the agency. All fees that it collects are deposited in the General Fund of the state, and the Texas Legislature then appropriates to the agency its operating budget. Thus, while a portion of the agency's customers, the real estate industry, provides the budget, the agency is answerable to the Legislature.

Before the agency first participated in the 1994–1995 SOE, it had developed a problem that was causing considerable concern for its three constituencies: the real estate industry, the public, and members of the Legislature. Much of the problem seemed to be that the demands of the industry and the population of the state had simply outgrown the leadership and culture of the Commission. In 1994 the board of the Commission hired a new executive director, William Kuntz, who was not from the real estate industry. Kuntz had a background in the securities field and had most recently been an employee in the Attorney General's Office. One of his first hires was a new director of human resources, Brian Frances, who had worked with Kuntz at the Attorney General's Office. Kuntz and Frances quickly concluded that a radical cultural change was an imperative for the organization. Kuntz developed a description of the agency, saying that, given its view of itself and its technology, it was one of the state's "Third World agencies." By that, Kuntz meant that the organization had relatively little pride in its mission with substantial deficiencies in its office resources and general technical equipment. It had a severely limited budget and a culture that seemed to emphasize that there was little hope of things getting better. Kuntz has a striking illustration of the degree of defeatism that he saw characterizing the organization. Over the years, the agency had collected a number of surveys of customers and staff. However, leadership chose not to open the boxes and analyze the results. They simply sat unopened in the agency file room on a top shelf. Apparently, the organization suspected that the surveys would simply be bad news that would depress everyone even more. While there clearly had been a crisis in the organization for years, there was no vision on how to improve the organization.

Kuntz and Frances seized upon the 1994–1995 SOE data as one way to start a change in the culture of the organization. When they received the results, the information confirmed that employees agreed with the agency's board and the constituents: the organization was in bad shape. Nevertheless, Kuntz and Frances broke tradition by bringing the bad news out into the open. Through a series of town hall meetings with all the staff of the organization, they carefully reviewed the data question by question. They next used the twenty constructs to set in motion a series of activities to directly address the problems that staff identified in responses to the survey. Then for the next two years specific projects were created that related directly to the areas identified by agency employees. In some cases, the agency needed more resources, and Kuntz had some limited success in increasing the level of the budget. In most cases, though, the improvements came not through more resources but from the inventiveness of an invigorated organization. The proof of the two years of work was illustrated by the 1996 SOE results. When the agency received the data, Brian ran whooping out into the hall. Shortly afterwards a general town meeting was held to review the results. Table 4 presents the data that the agency compiled and distributed at the town hall meeting.

One of the most remarkable things about the data is that the organization shows improvement on every one of the twenty constructs. Leadership that has a vision, an ability to communicate the vision and get the involvement of everyone, and data to track the movements are the ingredients for change. Some changes were far greater than others. Supervisor Effectiveness, Fairness, Employment Development, and Change Oriented showed tremendous improvements. Fair Pay and Benefits, each less under the control of leadership, showed the lowest amount of improvement.

What now should be the next step for this organization?[6] Has it reached its maximum level of quality and excellence? No, not at all! Truly high scores on any construct will be greater than 400, so there is much room left for advancement. Moreover, with growth and changing demands, the organization will find that it will be challenging to hold on to the hard-fought ground gained in the last two years. However, the organization has learned that it can change, and the organization itself may be the agent of improvement. Indeed, the groundwork seems well in place for the kind of continuous improvement that characterizes high-performing organizations.

Using the Survey with an Agency Board: State Board of Nurse Examiners

The State Board of Nurse Examiners has participated in the SOE for the last two state bienniums, evolving how it uses the survey. Initially it used the information as a barometer of current employee satisfaction with state employment at the agency. It also used some custom questions to gather information on specific organizational problems. Mostly this was a compliance use of the SOE.

Many employees in some of the smaller agencies in Texas feel that they are rarely "heard" in Texas state government. Perhaps this is the most valuable aspect of the survey for SBNE employees. They view the SOE as an instrument to share their concerns with the state leadership about their workplace and the state as an employer. The SBNE has also utilized SOE results for internal improvements. Results were

Table 4. Real Estate Commission Use of the SOE for Organizational Interventions

	1994–95	Selected Interventions	1996–97	% Change
Dimension I: Team				
Supervisor Effectiveness	228	Employee Handbook	308	35.09
Fairness	229	Myers-Briggs Team	298	30.13
Team Effectiveness	272	Building	329	20.96
Job Satisfaction	287	Employee of Quarter	337	17.42
Diversity	287	Award	330	14.98
		Comprehensive Cross Training		
Dimension II: Physical Work Settings				
Fair Pay	269	Wellness Program	284	5.58
Adequacy of Physical		Risk Management		
Environment	285	Program	340	19.3
Benefits	383	Administrative Leave	393	2.61
Employment		for outstanding		
Development	245	performance	324	32.24
		Risk Management related acquisitions		
Dimension III: General Organizational Features				
Change Oriented	261	Continuous Improve-	345	32.18
Goal Oriented	303	ment Initiative	358	18.15
Holographic	264	Program (CI^2)	324	22.72
Strategic Orientation	358	Change Management	394	10.06
Quality	323	Seminar	364	12.69
		Three-tiered employee participation in strategic planning		
Dimension IV: Communication Patterns				
Internal Communication	254	Town Meetings	313	23.23
Availability of		Survey of Organiza-		
Information	279	tional Excellence	305	9.32
External Communication	295	Technological	355	20.34
		Advancements: Internet, TRECFax, Voice-mail, and E-mail		
		Strategic Plan		
		Legislative Updates to employees		

Table 4. *(continued)*

	1994–95	Selected Interventions	1996–97	% Change
Dimension V: Personal Demands				
Time and Stress		Stress Management		
Management	288	Training	357	23.96
Burnout	263	Grievance Procedures	336	27.76
Empowerment	254	Wellness Program	302	18.9
		Employee Assistance		
		Program		
		Comprehensive Cross		
		Training		
		Continuous Improve-		
		ment Initiative		
		Program (CI^2)		

released to employees during a presentation attended by all employees, and employee quality circles have been formed to work on areas identified in the survey as needing improvement.

Between the 1994–1995 and 1996–1997 surveys, the agency underwent many changes, including hiring a new executive director, moving to a different location, and continued high staff turnover. This year the SBNE began to use the SOE data to provide information to the organization's board about problems and progress toward agency goals. Survey data have helped agency leadership, employees, and the agency itself develop joint perspectives on agency goals and plans. The inclusion of SOE information as part of the strategic plan that the agency must submit to the state is seen as a sure way to continue to develop its human resources.

More Case Study Information

These illustrations of how the SOE is used to build organizational excellence are some of the many other experiments underway. These findings are a common ground about which consensus can be developed on strengths of the organizations and priorities for improvement. Using such internal data is a proven method of mobilizing the members of the organization to set goals and achieve change. The SOE

Web site (www.utexas.edu/depts/sswork/survey) provides continuous updates of activities by organizations using the SOE.

Emerging Strategic Partnerships

Part of the development of new organizations that effectively increase quality and continuously create new products and services is the movement toward strategic alliances or partnerships. Commercial enterprises have learned that the model of owning and controlling all aspects of a business too often leads to a mediocre product with low rates of innovation. Strategic alliances permit an organization to focus on one thing or a limited number of things that it can do well and then have partners and suppliers that bring other needed dimensions. It is a clear alternative to the centralized, all-functions-under-the-same-tent mentality that often characterized business and government during much of this century. The process of creating partnerships is underway as Texas government changes and as leadership seeks to accelerate change and improve quality.

The Governor's Centers at the LBJ School of Public Affairs

Strategic alliances characterize the development of the SOE. While the main SOE office is housed in one academic unit at the University of Texas at Austin, specific resources to assist organizations in improving quality come from other directions. An important resource for state government is the Governor's Executive Development Program and the Governor's Center for Management Development. The Executive Development Program was originally created at the Lyndon B. Johnson School of Public Affairs on the University of Texas at Austin campus, while the Center for Management Development began in the Governor's Office. Both centers have now existed for several years on the University campus at the LBJ School. The centers are under the direction of Assistant Dean Barry Bales. Dr. Bales collaborates closely with us and utilizes SOE data to forecast content of training and technical assistance. Barry, in turn, has been instrumental in bringing the SOE to the attention of officials at the State Auditor's Office. They have extended the functions of the State Auditor from examinations of expenditure patterns to a full human resources audit that focuses on best uses and best practices for using and improving human resources. The State Auditor uses the SOE as one constant across agencies. Indeed, in the first assessment of human resource management for the state, the State Auditor stressed that in the most recent year (1996) at least 25 percent of state expenditures was for human resources (salary, benefits, training, etc.). The report calls for much greater attention to planning and full uses of these resources. All three of our offices are in regular contact with the Governor's Office of Budget and Planning and the Legislative Budget Office. The Legislative Budget Office began in 1996 requiring all state agencies to include in their strategic plans specific measures of human resource needs and detailing of specific interventions to address identified needs.

The size of the state's workforce and the amount of resources that the state expends for these jobs underscore the importance of fully utilizing the human resources of the state. In 1997 the total number of state positions topped 266,000, which represents about 3 percent of the total labor pool in the state.[7]

Throughout the process of achieving improvement in state government has been the recognition that the economic foundation of all of Texas must change. While agriculture and oil remain important in the state, most of the new jobs created since the severe economic problems of the late 1980s have been in knowledge industries. These are the fields of insurance, finance, education, international trade, health care, and high technology. What began markedly in the 1980s must continue to accelerate in the coming decades to provide for a robustly growing, yet worrisomely undereducated population. Here strategic alliances between business, education, and government are of critical importance. The influence of such alliances is strong in the development of the SOE and continues through the efforts of the Corporate Benchmarking Committee.

Missouri Focuses on Urban Areas

Professor Michael Kelly is using the SOE with a number of organizations in Missouri. He has worked with the SOE since its inception and through his teaching at the University of Missouri in Columbia has introduced it to organizations in that state. He has applied the SOE in Kansas City and St. Louis with organizations that are using a number of interventions to improve responsiveness and accountability. He also uses the SOE as an assessment tool with students working in a variety of social agencies as a means of understanding organizational properties and selecting strategies to improve quality. Professor Kelly teaches a joint class with us at our campus that uses the World Wide Web to make lectures, data, exercises, and instrumentation simultaneously available to graduate students in both Austin, Texas, and Columbia, Missouri. He has also made this course available to other smaller colleges in the Midwest through his university's extension program. Colleges may participate in the course by subscribing to it through Missouri's programs.

Connections with the Quality Movement in Industry and the Community

Another alliance is a joint collaboration of the University of Texas at Austin, the Austin Chamber of Commerce, and several of the largest high-technology companies in Austin—IBM, Motorola, and 3M. Together they founded in 1991 the Greater Austin Quality Council. The council sponsors the Baldridge Award competition for business, education, and government and through the University's Quality Center provides a continuous resource for training in fundamental quality procedures.

Such developments are another part of the environment in which the SOE has come into existence. There is a growing recognition in government, business, academic, and community service sectors that collaborations across sectors solves problems and increases excellence in ways that are not possible through isolated approaches. If businesses are to have healthy, well-educated, and motivated employees, governmental and community institutions such as health facilities, schools, public safety organizations, and universities must operate with standards of high quality. If government is to have the financial and social resources to meet its goals, then it must have highly educated and committed citizens and successful businesses in the community. Together these various participants represent the gradual shift in all sectors of the community to a vision of change, involvement, quality, and strategic alliances.

7 | How the Pursuit of Quality Undermines the Mass Production / Bureaucratic Model

The experience of holding a job and going to work each day has been greatly influenced by three inventions and the struggle to tame a defeated adversary after the Second World War. Each of these has shaped our personal lives and our communities and collectively made today's world radically different for leaders that seek to create better organizations. The survey process as detailed in this book is one of the tools of organization transformation mandated through these inventions. The inventions, moreover, have also created a new challenge for all organizations and public life in general.

Figuring out the best way to get work done has a long history of attempts and speculation. For much of human existence what one did and how one related to others was controlled by cultural patterns that were likely unrecognized by members of the culture. In the distant past, with human settlements small and isolated, the opportunity to see and compare how others did things was limited. Thus, people were likely to conclude that the local arrangements, whatever they might be, were the only way possible. However, population growth, innovations in communications technology, mass migrations from rural areas to urban centers, and the successes of modern farming and manufacturing have produced very different ways for people to live and work. Working for wages, being supervised and supervising others, urban living, the concept of retirement, high levels of consumption, encountering choice in kind of work, places to live, and sources of information and entertainment are profoundly new experiences for millions.

Intensive agriculture culminating with heavy use of technology and a declining use of human labor is the first invention that altered life and how work is done in this century. This new way of living and working produced modern mass society, a society of workers and consumers. This is also a society not of thousands of individuals, as in traditional society, but of tens of millions. Mass society came into being by with the change of how work is defined, how workers are trained, and where workers live.

When Individuals Controlled Work and Quality

How things were made at the start of the current century remained quite constant for more than a millennium. Knowledge of how to do or make a particular thing was the possession of a skilled craftsman. When the artisan sought to transfer skills to another person, it was through a years-long mentoring process whereby the novitiate learned by following the example of the craftsman. Little of the knowledge and skill was written. The tools of the trade were crucial and kept as the individual possessions of the craftsman.[1]

Clearly, the craft approach ensured that how something was made, the thing's quality, beauty, and handiness were all very much under the control of the individual craftsman or of a few people in a small shop. Such a method of manufacturing was, in itself, not resistant to innovation, but except for the ingenuity of an individual artisan, other conditions that might spur innovation were weak. With communities small, travel difficult, and written communications tedious, there was scant opportunity to view a competitor's work and likewise a low likelihood that a customer might comparison-shop among artisans. Thus the conditions of small, somewhat isolated craft shops, a slow "hands-on" method of training new artisans, and primitive travel and communication conditions meant a slow pace of innovation in what was made as well as how things were made.

Making the Organization, Not the Individual, Responsible for the Work

What changed all of this was industrialization. It moved the authority for the control of work from the individual to the organization. Industrialization was clearly apparent in the eighteenth century in England and France in the looming of textiles and building of machinery. Other countries of Europe and the colonial Americans eagerly sought such secrets of manufacturing. Moving at first slowly and then exploding in Western Europe and the United States, work in complex organizations, the factory, pushed aside the individual-centered and controlled-craft approach. *This change in how things are manufactured via the factory is the second invention that contributes immensely to how work is done today.*

How the Model T Created the Model Bureaucracy

The example most enshrined in the folklore of the Industrial Age is the factory of the automobile manufacturer, Henry Ford. Ford, like thousands of his contemporaries, was a backyard mechanic and tinkerer who was fascinated by the prospect of a self-propelled carriage. Contemporaries of Ford were absorbed in the thousands of design alternatives that exist at the dawn of a new technology. Where should the engine be located? How many wheels should be on the carriage? How best do you spark or ignite the fuel in the cylinder? How do you transfer power from the engine to the wheels? How do you lubricate and cool the motor? While Ford experimented with these concerns, he also investigated other dimensions of making the car that would prove to unleash a revolution in how all organizations were put together.

Ultimately the genius of Ford lay not in tinkering with the mechanical components of the automobile but in a radically different approach to handling the layout of all the work needed to produce the automobile. Rather than hiring craftsmen to build his cars so that each man produced a single automobile, Ford divided the process of building a car into hundreds of separate, discrete, but linked tasks. He then positioned workers in an actual line to do each of these tasks. As a worker completed a task, rather than beginning a different task, he passed the item that he was working on to the person adjacent to him, who accomplished the next task. The first worker simply secured another piece of raw material and repeated his original task. Thus, work became repeating the same task and passing the partially finished item when the task was completed to the next worker. Rather than having the workers hand the task to the next man, Ford placed the part or partial automobile on a moving conveyer belt that moved the gradually evolving product from worker to worker. Thus, both the definition and control of the production process passed from the individual worker to the organization. The assembly line, the proxy of management, set the pace and routine of work. This means of manufacturing became known as the *assembly line method, scientific management,* or *Fordism.*[2] Through the evangelism of men like Ford and Frederick W. Taylor, it became the preferred means of manufacturing things.[3]

Assembly line manufacturing excels at three things. One is high volume at low cost. The second is being able to make extremely complicated things involving thousands of processes and parts. The third is building such complex products with relatively unskilled labor.

Reasons for the Predominance of the Model

The success of the assembly line model is undeniable. Ford's procedures were quickly adopted and extended. The major popularizer of the concept and scholar of the method, Frederick W. Taylor, testified before many bodies and urged all business enterprises to adopt *scientific management,* Taylor's term for the assembly line approach.

While the approach produced wealth, it had clear disadvantages for traditional skilled workers. Such workers were often put out of work by a factory that could build things with cheaper, unskilled labor. Working conditions in factories were often shocking, and many supervisors or foremen treated workers like machines.

However, as U.S. industry adopted the model, American productivity soon set the pace for the world. The uniqueness and inherent superiority of this approach to manufacturing made the U.S. economy the strongest in the world. It proved pivotal in the defeat of American enemies in both world wars and weighed heavily in the collapse of the Soviet Union and the end of the Cold War.

The assembly line method quickly made available large numbers of high-quality yet low-cost goods. Moreover, through work simplification it both created a demand for unskilled and semiskilled labor and provided handsome rewards to such labor. Regular laborers rather than just scarce and expensive artisans became well-compensated employees.

Assembly line work created a tremendous new demand for labor. Rapid job growth in the factories drew surplus agricultural labor from farms, creating cities and producing an urban, then suburban, middle class. Soon agriculture, increasingly lacking cheap and available labor, became more mechanized and factorylike with large corporate-style businesses replacing family farms. While the methods of manufacturing created a wealthy elite of the factory owners, the factory jobs transformed millions of impoverished migrants and agricultural workers into middle-class homeowners. The factory system thus both created wealth and redistributed significant portions to the population.[4]

Regular pay and indoor work as a replacement for the more demanding agricultural field labor caused important changes in the society. Villages grew quickly into towns and then cities as manufacturers increased the size of facilities and required more workers. Now with regular incomes, the workers themselves became a market for the abundance of goods that the new manufacturing process created. Thus, assembly line manufacturing was an important cause of the transformation of American society from a world of small, largely self-sufficient farms and independent producers to urban centers with middle-class workers employed by large organizations.

The significant genius of Ford was not the Model A or Model T but how the cars were made. *This is our second invention that helped make today's world of work.* Ford provided the world a model of an organization that broke work into small, visible, linear processes. He provided a clear illustration of how supervision could be used to direct unskilled labor.

These two inventions, intensive farming and factories, which were actually the results of thousands of innovations, changed work, the individual, and the community. Western Europe and the United States were the first large-scale participants in this change. Japan came next. The adoption of the two inventions has continued to move inexorably from culture to culture for the entire twentieth century.

Signs of Discontent

Yet the core strength of the model (its utilization of unskilled and semiskilled people governed through uniform impersonality, work specification, and the control of the assembly line) generated problems. These problems were developing even as the method swept all manufacturing in the early twentieth century. Among them were worker unrest and frustration with the tedium and exhaustion of working on the assembly line. The constraints and demands of the assembly line required workers to stand at one place for long hours performing the same task repeatedly. Worker absences or even breaks from work to get a drink or go to the bathroom had to be approved by management to maintain the flow of work on the line. Moreover, since workers could be hired and made productive with brief training, there was little incentive to provide long tenure for workers or to increase wages. Indeed, if labor supplies were ample, employees could be viewed as part of the material of the factory process. Factory owners would seek material at the lowest price possible to maximize profits, and this included seeking the lowest labor costs.

In no small degree, the union movements that parallel the rise of scientific management were in response to the sort of organizational leadership and work conditions occasioned by the assembly line method. By simplifying work and making the worker a commodity much like the raw materials, workers became alienated from the work and the organization. By hiring, then dismissing workers in response to market demand, changing methods of manufacturing, and opportunities in the labor market, wary distrust and sharp antagonism developed toward managers and owners.[5] Such outcomes were clearly contrary to the visions of proselytizers such as Taylor and Ford.

How the Telephone Rescued Scientific Management

Soon both employee frustration and employee motivation became substantial management concerns. The next great shift in thinking of how to create organizations came with a bit of serendipity that was associated with the third invention contributing to how we work today. *The invention was the telephone. However it was not the telephone, but how best to manufacture it, that contributed so significantly to modern workplaces.*

There are two parts to what this invention unearthed about how to create an organization. The first part involved two Harvard Business School researchers, F. J. Roethlisberger and W. J. Dickson, who were conducting research in the manufacturing arm of American Telephone and Telegraph's Western Electric. From a series of experiments and contrary to their initial hypotheses, the researchers were surprised to find physical working conditions and pay were *not* the major motivations of the worker. Rather, how the workers felt they were perceived by the organization or, more directly, management seemed more adequately to account for motivation. If workers felt they were valued and appreciated by management, they worked harder and produced more with better quality. If they felt slighted by management, they produced less with poorer quality.

From this finding came a very different emphasis on how the organization should relate to the worker. Under the assembly line model, the worker was viewed as an element in the manufacturing process. The worker was viewed as another component, just as a lathe, drill, or grinder might be. Management's responsibility was to set the precise tasks before the worker and closely supervise the work and the output.

What came of Roethlisberger and Dickson's inquiries was a new management emphasis on providing workers the needed tools for a task and then letting the workers decide how best to do the task. This orientation came to be called the *human relations* movement. It directed management's attention not to the product and how to logically lay out the work to create the product, but rather how best to satisfy the worker. This method assumed that most workers were naturally productive and creative and more knowledgeable about their work than was management. Management's concerns should be directed toward assisting workers to be productive and ensuring that recognition and appreciation were afforded the workers. While the focus of the assembly line method was on the steps in producing the product, the focus of human relations was on the psychological well-being of the worker.

Crises Set the Stage for the Second Part of the Telephone's Contribution

During the 1960s an accumulation of events began to augur an immense shift in how organizations, large and small, were to be structured and directed. That decade began with immense and corrosive social and political issues that reached a breaking point in the late years of the Johnson administration. One great issue was the direction and pursuit of the Vietnam War.[6]

A second great issue was the urban unrest in black communities in the cities and the alienation of youth on the nation's campuses. Both phenomena came to challenge the morality and legitimacy of business and government alike. These two large issues cast a darkening gloom over social discourse and raised deep questions about whether the American experiment in democratic participation and full participation of all had now finally run its course.

An additional surprising contribution to the gloom came from the loss of control by American entities of the pricing of imported oil with the emergence of the Organization of Petroleum Exporting Countries (OPEC) cartel. This group of countries, largely from the Middle East, wrestled control of production and pricing from international companies such as Texaco, Shell, Exxon, and Chevron in the early 1970s and began to dictate supply and price levels to the United States. OPEC mandated rapid increases in prices of petroleum feed stocks. This caused a variety of consumer and commercial products such as gasoline, fuel oil, and other derivatives like fertilizers and plastics to skyrocket in price. Quickly American consumers faced escalating energy costs, long lines at gasoline stations, and even the inability to purchase fuel.

Such problems led automobile buyers to search for vehicles that used less fuel. European and Japanese companies, long accustomed to far higher gasoline prices, responded by importing autos to the United States and established important consumer beachheads. This assault on the American auto market began even as the Japanese were eliminating American producers in consumer electronics, including watches, radios, televisions, and video recorders. They were moving in a threatening fashion to do the same in commodity memory chips for computer gear and machine tools in factories, just as they had done in watches and hand calculators in the 1960s.

Even as the American economy and the consumer adjusted to higher oil prices (and as gasoline prices began to decline), American auto producers discovered that consumers continued to prefer foreign goods, particularly Japanese. The reason for this preference, as became painfully clear, was that Japanese products were of higher quality. There were fewer defects in new products, durability was greater, improvements came more frequently, and the degree of fit and finish was superior.[7] Moreover, the rate of innovation leading to improvement in quality among Japanese companies was greater than what American producers were achieving.

By the 1990s consumer electronics were totally dominated by the Japanese, and Japanese automobile manufacturers were setting the world standards for quality. Both Honda and Toyota were vying with General Motors and Ford to produce the best-selling American sedan. Toyota, known in the 1970s for producing "one size fits all, cookie-cutter econoboxes," astounded the automotive world in 1991 when its new Lexus displaced the Mercedes and the BMW as the world's highest-quality automobile. The manufacture of the automobile, which in many ways set the paradigm of how to create the modern organization and was largely the great domain of American "know-how," was turning to the leadership of another culture. That culture, Japan, had entered the field late, yet clearly bettered the best that America could offer. This was a shock to automobile manufacturers and to the culture itself, for Americans felt they led the world in building the most productive and creative organizations.[8]

A Culture of Responsibility and Participation

In the 1980s and 1990s scholars of business organizations found that Japanese workers seemed to be more responsible than American workers and more eager to see that improvements were made in products.

Indeed studies of Japanese workers indicated far higher levels of suggestions by workers within the company to improve the company's product. Some studies indicated that a typical Japanese worker might stop the assembly line a hundred or a thousand times more often than the American counterpart. The stops occurred when the worker saw a flaw in the product or how the product might be improved. Whereas the Japanese worker saw an obligation to correct a flawed product and anticipated company approval, the American worker did not see this function as his or her responsibility. Moreover, the American worker anticipated criticism if he or she stopped the assembly line to suggest an improvement.

It appeared that Japanese companies had greater concerns and superior mechanisms to ensure quality in their processes. For example, one researcher found that among room air conditioner manufacturers Japanese manufacturers had a defect rate nearly 70 times lower. Similarly, service call rates after manufacture were only about 7 percent that of their American counterparts. The gains coming from workers being concerned and involved with improvement in Japanese companies were substantial, and examples were found in many fields.

These data supported the notion that the Japanese worker was more concerned with the quality of work and felt a greater sense of ownership in the company than the American worker. Such findings surprised and alarmed many Americans. This led to questions about why quality seemed so much better established in many Japanese companies. Additional questions asked why Japanese workers were so much more sensitive to the concern for quality than American workers were.

As many observers have pointed out, culture provides part of the explanation. Japan, unlike the United States, is a densely populated country with over 100 million people all residing in an area no larger than the state of California. Consequently, the need to recognize how one's actions affect one's neighbor is much more paramount than in the United States, where there are far greater opportunities for isolation and less experience in recognizing how one's actions may have an immediate impact on one's neighbors. A land of small, interlocking rice farms requires more social consideration than a land of open, endless horizons.

Pearl Harbor as the Trigger for the Japanese Quality Revolution

Other forces also were important in creating the concern for quality that characterized many Japanese products. Clearly much of the success of modern-day Japanese manufacturing can be traced back to

American experts and American efforts to improve quality and lessen authoritarianism that came to Japan after World War II. Much of American concern during the occupation of Japan after its defeat in 1945 was how to end the feudal shogun structures that characterized much of Japanese life. Such authoritarian entities were felt to be much of the driving force that created the totalitarian regime that attacked the United States in 1941 at Pearl Harbor. Douglas MacArthur, the military governor during the occupation period, sought to install democratic reforms in Japanese public and private life. His leadership proved to be especially profound in their impact on Japanese manufacturing by encouraging Japan to make the most of the best of American know-how.

The Rest of the Telephone Story

Among the experts who came to Japan after the war was W. Edwards Deming, a statistician, who was steeped in quality concerns as they had developed in America during and after World War II.[9] Deming is also the link to the second part of the invention of the telephone and how the manufacture of the telephone led to an important issue in how to create modern organizations. Deming had met an earlier proponent of quality, W. A. Shewhart, and was greatly impressed by his writings. Shewhart was an employee of Bell Laboratories and had written in 1931 *Economic Control of Quality of Manufactured Product,* which established many of the tools and techniques that are used today to ensure quality. Shewhart emphasized that management could take clear steps to improve quality by setting clear standards and sampling from the product flow to determine whether production was within quality parameters.

During most of the twentieth century, telephone service in the United States was provided by a single company, American Telephone and Telegraph (AT&T). It was one of the century's most successful monopolies. It built telephones, switching gear, strung telephone poles and landlines, and provided local and long distance service. Since the company made its own equipment, it knew the value of equipment that was very durable and had a minimum of flaws. Equipment failures cost the company dearly, and there were continuous efforts to improve the quality of manufacture. So important were AT&T's quality improvements that two of the most recognizable names in quality, Deming and Juran, were directly schooled in the ideas of quality through experiences coming from AT&T.

Building upon ideas developed from AT&T's experiences, Deming offered several principles that he described as the path to quality. He worked for years as a consultant in both Japan and the United States assisting companies that were receptive to adopting such principles. In the early years it was particularly Japanese companies that listened closely to Deming.

Years later, when he was approached by American companies that had heard of Deming through the successes of Japanese competitors, he offered these same principles. He felt the principles would assure American manufacturers of being able to compete with the Japanese just as they had changed Japanese manufacturing. Having played a role in transforming Japan to the quality model, Deming felt confident that Americans could learn to change their organizational culture as well.

A few consistent themes cut through these principles. They focus on urging a belief in the importance of quality. Moreover, quality is viewed not as an end but a continuous pursuit, and change is seen as continuous. Deming emphasized that the change process can be initiated and maintained only through visionary leadership; and that teamwork, full organizational participation and empowerment of the employee, and continuous training must be part of the life of the worker.

Another of Deming's peers and almost as influential in defining this new era of organizations is Joseph Juran.[10] Juran, like Shewhart, was a quality inspector for AT&T in the Hawthorne plant of Western Electric.[11] Like Deming, Juran called for a commitment to quality and emphasized planning, controlling work to meet plans, and employee participation. He emphasized even more vigorously than Deming that success can only be based upon customer satisfaction. He advocated the use of surveys and market research to ascertain customer needs and perceptions of the product or service.

A third major voice in the quality movement is Philip Crosby.[12] Crosby is best known for his view that "quality is free." Quality means doing things right the first time, thus reducing the costs of reworking products, issuing callbacks, and eliminating inventories of repair parts and defective merchandise. Crosby's principles were largely in agreement with those of Deming and Juran; his special contribution was the argument that the pursuit of quality means a less costly product. This was an important rejoinder to critics who claimed that such an emphasis on quality creates more expensive products than those produced with conventional approaches.

Core Teachings from the Quality Movement

The *quality* method is unlike the *assembly line* method, which focused on the layout of work to manufacture a product, or *human relations,* which focused on the motivations and psychological states of the worker. The quality method emphasizes the customer and steps to improve the satisfaction of the customer with the product or service. It appears with a number of labels, including Total Quality Management (TQM), Continuous Quality Improvement (CQI), and Quality Management (QM). This new method has at its core several principles that seem to characterize the teachings of its proponents and the practices of the adherents. These principles are as follows:

• Products and services do not exist as static entities but rather are processes inherently susceptible to change and thus improvement.

• Change in the quality of a product or service can only come from organizations fully understanding all parts of the process of creating the good or service.

• Improvement cannot be simply secured by dictum from the top. Rather, it must include the active participation of all persons involved in the organization.

• The pursuit of quality begins and continues only through visionary leadership that can effectively call forth and mobilize the best efforts of everyone in the organization.

• Work itself must be seen as a team process, and all workers must develop skills to work effectively in teams.

• It is less expensive to emphasize quality; only the pursuit of quality can ensure the long-term viability of the organization.

• Change is continuous, and structures must be created to support the continued education and development of members of the organization.

• Quality means honesty, integrity, and dependability in all actions internal and external to the organization. Employee fears of being honest or fear of participating must be driven from the organization.

• Quality is achieved only from being close to the customer, listening to the customer, and seeking to meet the needs of the customer.

• Quality, continuous improvement, and high levels of employee participation must become central norms, the core tenets of the organization. All must be watchful for hollow slogans that substitute empty declarations for vigorous, dedicated action.

America's defeat of Japan in World War II brought the ideas of quality to Japan that were pioneered in the manufacture of the telephone. The concepts of quality flourished in Japan and contributed significantly to aspects of Japan's industrial culture. The sudden rise in the price of oil created a market for thrifty Japanese cars; cars and consumer electronics provided two avenues by which the Japanese introduced higher-quality products to Americans and the world.

Understanding the Rising Demand for Quality

The workplace and organizations in the wealthiest and most powerful countries of the world today owe much to the inventions of intensive agriculture, the automobile, and the telephone. The successes of modern agriculture made it possible for the work of one farmer to feed hundreds of others. This, in turn, made cities possible and created available labor that could be applied to work in factory settings.

Henry Ford's factory became the model of how to organize work in the modern era. Factory settings have showed the world how complex products can be made at low cost and provided a model to train and develop workers much more successfully than the older craft approach. So successful has the factory model been that it has been exported to service organizations, and today government agencies, education, health, and welfare entities are cast much in the mold of factory organizations.

AT&T's concern for successful manufacturing broadened understandings about the employee and to an extent made the employee a bit less of a commodity than under Ford's organizational model. Acute observers in Japan of AT&T's progress quickly adapted those tools to Japan. This profoundly changed Japanese manufacturing, and the Japanese launched throughout the world what has come to be known as a "quality revolution."

In this revolution organizations are advised to listen carefully to customers, and employees are called upon to think and have a sense of ownership in what they do. This engenders continuous change and improvement results. This process transforms a static bureaucracy into an organization where everyone thinks and innovates. Thus, thinking organizations are created.

Once a given company starts down this path, competitors must follow, or they will quickly be in trouble. Revolution is an apt term, and the rate of change, competition, and innovation now touches almost every area of the private sector of the world's economies.

The organization that successfully pursues quality cannot help but change the fundamentals of the equation between employer and the organization that held sway during the factory period.

Moreover, the role of these three inventions (intensive agriculture, the factory, and the telephone) and the impact of the quality revolution are not limited to manufacturing settings. The principles of this quality revolution are striking in their clarity, in their consonance with larger, fundamental cultural values of American democratic society, and in their implications for organizations beyond manufacturing. A fundamental change in American businesses has set the stage for serious thought about the need to improve quality in all reaches of American life.

As the twentieth century winds down, so do the organizations, public and private, that were created from the innovations and wealth of the mass production era. These organizations were built upon high levels of specialization, hierarchical control, relative constancy of product or service, and a predictable external environment. However, rapidly changing environments and increasing competition have rendered the old formula of volume production and mass scale ineffective in area after area of the American economy. Now competition and a more sophisticated consumer produce a demand for products and services that respond to consumer expectations centered upon standards of high quality. Moreover, the quality model is one of continuous change and improvement. The product or service that is the standard this year slips to the middle of the pack by the second year.

This rising call for quality cannot be met through a redoubling of efforts to continue with the old paradigm of assembly line manufacture. Instead energies must be directed toward a different paradigm, and the creation of that paradigm requires establishing the conditions that permit the growth of quality.

This organizational inheritance has been provided at the end of a century of great progress and change. Through intensive agriculture only a small percentage of the members of any community are engaged in the production of food. Most individuals support themselves not by working for themselves but for organizations. With their emphasis on consistency and low cost, organizations, not individuals, have proven to be a superior way of providing goods and services. Our schools, businesses, governmental agencies, churches, and even recreational choices all follow the same patterns of using formal organizations as the means for reaching goals.

The highly structured formal organization in which decision making is reserved for the organizational hierarchy has these advantages:

134

- Consistency and uniformity of product or service
- Relatively low cost
- The ability to use people with little training or education to perform labor

Alternatively, it has these disadvantages:

- Tailored or individualized products or services cannot be produced or, if produced, do not have the low cost associated with mass produced articles or services.
- Change comes slowly since the hierarchy of the organization typically isolates decision makers from those who are engaged in much of the production process as well as the end user of the product or service.
- Improvements in quality and innovation are suppressed by the hierarchical nature of decision making and the alienation created with employees.

Summary

In manufacturing the quality revolution has made it impossible to continue with many of the core principles of the assembly line model. The traditional assembly line model was based upon the authority of the organization to decide what was to be done and how to do it. Change came only slowly, mostly from the top down to the lower levels. Individuals were not hired to innovate or think. Indeed, innovation other than at the top was a problem.

The demands of the quality revolution, though, require change and improvement at all levels in the organization and throughout the production process. Rather than being an organization where only a few think and design, everyone must be thinking and involved in the continuous improvement process. Involvement, participation, thinking, personal accountability, all were values started by the factory model. They are, however, necessary requisites for any organization moving into the quality world.

The quality revolution carries the seeds of undoing the hierarchical organizational world (the factory model) that is the preeminent design of not just business but also modern society. Change, innovation, and closeness to the customer create private organizations that are lean, nimble, and much less hierarchical than Ford or AT&T could ever envision at their peaks. Technology permits organizations to be much more virtual. The factory floor and the office cubicle are giving way to telephones, laptops, and modems. As these changes continue in the private sector, they clearly have great implications for the public sector and the private lives of employees and citizens.

These changes that have gotten underway in the worlds of manufacturing, retail, and distribution are starting to explode in all other areas of society. The implications of this trend are the subject of the next chapter.

8 | Creating the New Paradigm: Thinking Organizations

The previous chapter traces the pattern of how paradigms of social systems and formal organizations came into being and then were replaced during the nineteenth and twentieth centuries. Today fast-paced change, competition, and the growth of new technologies call for a different paradigm and thus different organizations. The use of the SOE is clearly part of a process of creating a different organization for a new social paradigm. These new organizations and members participating in them, with the high emphasis on quality, responsibility, and empowerment, in turn may make an important contribution to the community in which the person lives. This chapter delves more deeply into how thinking organizations are created and the impact such organizations may have upon the individual and the community.

The work of Deming, Crosby, Juran, and others provides us with technical procedures for increasing the quality of products and services. In some cases, the technical procedures require rigorous and exhaustive analysis of a production process so that mistakes and superfluous or redundant steps are removed. Flow charts, fishbone or cause and effect diagrams, Pareto charts, and scatter diagrams are examples of technical procedures associated with process improvement in the quality movement. Other specifics of the quality movement are less focused on discrete process improvements. Instead, the stress is on the creation of new social norms in the organization. These include increasing the power of persons at lower levels in the organization and leading through example rather than forced compliance. Everyone is urged to participate to continually increase quality. Every employee is urged to fully understand each work process and seek to find ways to improve the process. The new norms emphasize creating the highest sense of pride by members in the organization and the product.

Both the discrete technical steps and the new social norms are part of the route to establishing the quality paradigm in an organization. Quality requires commitment, a different way of doing things, and it involves much more than simply following old habits.

How Paradigms Shift

Why organizations become involved in the quality movement is usually the result of outside conditions that encourage or compel improvements in quality. In many cases, change occurs because of powerful threats to the existence of the organization, compelling the organization to search for different approaches. Events that disturb the status quo, such as the appearance of genuine competitors, can cause radical examination and change in an organization. Or the creation of market mechanisms that permit purchasers and consumers to compare and appraise quality and cost can result in organizational change. Change may result when there is a fundamental shift in the availability or cost of resources, or when new ideas and technologies effectively challenge the dominance of existing providers. Many of these external conditions now affect organizations everywhere and force them toward a radical examination of how an organization operates.

An important part of the shift for American organizations and communities comes from the increased globalization of labor. Manufacturing today is different in one critical way from the situation of perhaps fifteen years ago. It now occurs all over the world. For example, not long ago I bought a promotional watch at a national burger chain for less than two dollars. It is an electronic device that would have cost probably fifty dollars in 1980. The watch, the band, and the box—with a "Jurassic Park—The Lost World" logo were all labeled "Made in China." I suspect that the worker in that factory earned a daily wage less than what I paid for the hamburger, soda, and fries that I bought along with the watch. This world market of manufacturing creates a world market of labor where the manufacture of a given item gravitates to the regions that have the lowest marginal labor costs. Labor must either compete with the lowest-cost provider or offer special skills unmatched by cheaper markets.

The globalization of labor has served to increase the amount of service work in the high-cost labor markets of the United States, Western Europe, and Japan. The increase in service work is part of the worldwide migration of manual assembly labor to lower-cost, lesser-educated markets. The North American Free Trade Agreement (NAFTA) and the export engines of the less developed Asian countries, including China, are manifestations of this labor migration. Because of these open markets in America, service work is replacing manufacturing work as traditional jobs move to low-wage countries. Indeed service work is now the largest sector in the American job market. Service work has to absorb both new entrants into the labor force and persons who lose jobs in the manufacturing sector.

Service work can be divided into two basic categories. One is work that requires only minimum education but cannot be exported to lower-cost regions because the nature of the service involves an intangible, perishable, and immediate skill. Counter work at a fast food restaurant or routine nursing services in a medical setting are examples.

The second category of service work is knowledge work that requires high levels of education. The professions (law, medicine, engineering, architecture, teaching, social work, etc.), creative arts, computer software design, financial services, and the like are illustrations. Both types of service work are becoming the major source of employment in mature economies as traditional sources of employment in farming, mining, and industrial manufacturing provide far fewer jobs.

One other activity driving revolutionary, organizational change is the great gale of corporate downsizing, mergers, and the creation of new corporations that is underway. To a considerable degree, the old companies built around the principles of scientific management and mass production with large numbers of employees, acres of factory space, and workers with highly specialized and repetitive tasks are rapidly disappearing. Enterprises associated with steel, chemicals, autos, and railroads run with far fewer employees, only a fraction of the numbers of a scant twenty years ago. These industries utilize computer-assisted processes that eliminate both assembly line jobs and supervisory positions associated with old smokestack America. Banking, insurance, health care, transportation, and communications —the service industries—are also being shrunk, decentralized, and reinvented as far smaller and flexible. These organizational changes come with increased demands upon labor to learn new tasks and find better, faster, and cheaper ways of getting work done.

As jobs in America become service jobs, the desirable service jobs, those with high pay and benefits, are ones that demand "knowledge" workers. Knowledge workers do not perform the same task day in and day out. Rather these workers write, create, arrange new tasks, work in teams, and continually face the demands to be innovative and relate to new challenges, situations, customers, and competitors. Thinking organizations require creative, thoughtful employees. Change is critical for organizational survival and requires workers who can create the changing organization.

Major Dimensions of the New Paradigm

Interactions among formal organizations, their employees, and the larger community are creating new sets of relationships, such as working at home, job sharing, or day care at the work site. Functions once reserved for the public sector (mail delivery, welfare services, police work, prisons, elementary and secondary education) are being examined as candidates for privatization. Many federal government functions are being transferred to state and local levels of government, and all levels of government are seeking areas where they can move more of the responsibility to the individual. All these changes and experiments can be seen as beginning steps to construct a new paradigm to replace the old based upon the assembly line model.

Among the major tasks we face in developing this new paradigm are these:
• Bringing forth the requisite visionary leadership necessary to tackle the daunting challenges
• Transforming traditional static organizations into self-reflective, thinking organizations
• Creating entirely new organizations
• Establishing different psychological relationships between the individual and the organization
Let's examine these critical tasks in a bit of detail.

The Role of Visionary Leadership

Formal organizational change may start from any level within an organization, but if it is to succeed, it must have dedicated leadership from the very top of the organization. The leadership needed to build a new paradigm is very different from the leadership required to maintain a successful organization. The new leadership must first be attuned to what members of the organization are feeling and thinking. Additionally, the leadership must be equally close to what customers and clients expect. Several major areas of leadership requirements include

being willing to go beyond what currently satisfies customers,

demanding far higher levels of participation than is the comfortable norm in most organizations,

embracing the swift velocity of change, and

being able to bring diversity and cultural sophistication to the organization.

In the previous era of assembly line organization, leadership was often called upon simply to maintain and refine goals for an organization. This explains the use of the term *management*. Management means to organize, direct, and control. Once an organization hit upon a successful product or service, it could expect a product lifetime measured in decades before a successor threatened. Today products or services may have a lifetime measured in only months. Under these conditions the creation of new products or services is as vital as controlling and directing were for organizations under the old paradigm. Old hierarchical organizations seeking to make the transition to thinking organizations and newly created organizations need visionary and inspired leaders far more than they need managers. Visionary leadership includes being able to thrive in rapid and revolutionary change, not just presiding over a slow-moving ship.

While successful organizations must know who their customers are and what customers want, simply focusing on that theme is not an adequate assurance for long-term success. Sometimes the wellsprings of innovation are far from current needs of customers, and products and services are created when corresponding needs from customers are patently lacking.[1] The transistor, the integrated circuit, the personal computer, nylon, television, cellular telephones, and the Internet were as much technologies that then created markets as items that came from the manifest needs of customers. There are many illustrations of development preceding need. For example, many people seemingly use the desktop computer only as a replacement for the typewriter. They fail to see its potential as a communication, reference, and decision support device thousands of times more significant than the improved typewriter surrogate. The product waits for needs that many customers have yet to recognize.

141

Being close to customers is critical to refining and developing products that meet current needs. However, breakthroughs to new markets and radically new technologies seem to depart from the usual prescription of continuous, incremental improvement familiar to the quality movement. While it is important to recognize the role of the customer, some customers may be wrong.

Pursuing some customers may not be in the best interests of the organization. Organizations cannot be all things to all people. Choices have to be made to pursue some opportunities, some markets, while of course ignoring others. In a blunt way, Herb Kelleher, the head of Southwest Airlines, makes just this point by noting that serving some customers devalues the staff and quality goals of the organization.[2] He notes that there is the occasional customer that Southwest Airlines will not sell a seat to!

One of the most provocative principles of quality management and, indeed, a recurrent finding from human relations is the call for increased participation of employees in the decision making of the organization. While Frederick W. Taylor's writings called for the collaboration of management and workers, the day-to-day reality was different. In most complex organizations, constructed on the principles of Taylor's assembly line model, there is little opportunity for or even legitimacy to employee participation, and the phenomenon of the union movement in the United States was in response to the denial of participation. It is thus not surprising to find that one of the most difficult hurdles to overcome in moving into the quality model is to convince leadership in the organization to permit genuine participation. Perhaps puzzling but equally difficult is persuading employees to participate.

It is fair to ask why a company would want all employees to participate in organizational tasks. For the scientific management/assembly line model, participation was not desirable. This model operated from a perspective of "one best way." Usually that one best way was already known by top management, and what management wanted was for workers to do the work their way—management's way. The advance that human relations represents was to view the participation of workers as something that increases the morale of workers by making them feel wanted, more essential. This model then assumes that workers who feel wanted and valued will be better workers. While experience has supported this view, it nevertheless seems a little hollow or even manipulative. It is as if there is recognition that work in an assembly line world will generate some grit and friction. The friction causes needless wear, and participation can be added as a lubricant to make the machine run a bit more smoothly.

However, participation in the quality model comes from the realization that there is *not* a best way to get things done. There is only a path of continuing to work to do things better. Worker participation means everyone from all vantage points is working to improve the product or service. Participation is not a valued thing just in itself but part of the process of understanding and improvement.

Effective participation must be distinguished from participation, per se. Effective participation does not mean equal participation because talent, experience, energy, and education are never equally distributed. Effective participation is best understood by examining the particulars of a decision. For example, in an auto plant, a mechanical engineer might play the greater role in designing a particular gear assembly in a transmission. However, a line worker might play the larger role in determining how best to lay out the work and tools to build the gear assembly. In a police department the police chief might play the larger role in articulating a policy of community policing. However, an officer working a given beat might play the larger role in saying what hours should be worked or where to effectively communicate with youth or how to control gangs.[3]

The key to effective participation is to create an organization where all members know the mission and know that the goal is to arrive at the best possible decision, time after time. This implies that all members have the ability to know their own strengths and weaknesses. It means having members who know when to speak, when to listen, and when to support. Such conditions most readily emerge in smaller organizations and come into being only over months, extending into years to build such a culture. However, one sure measure of an organization that will find the pursuit of quality elusive is one where participation is given grudgingly or distributed with paternalism. Leaders who feel the burden of teaching employees how to participate while developing structures and policies to govern and control participation run a very grave risk. The risk is that of never achieving effective participation rather than of having the organization run amuck because of too much participation.

One of the first lessons that American companies learned from Japanese competitors was that quality meant continuously improving products. What would be "best of the breed" one year would be a mediocre contender the next. Manufacturers have had to shorten product life cycles from years to months. In the early 1960s, for example,

IBM introduced the Selectric typewriter and planned a product life cycle of fifty years. IBM knew that, as the product was conceived in the 1950s, it would have a strong market position in the 1960s and 1970s and then a declining period of market penetration into the next century. Now contrast this with the lifetime of computer hardware and software. Desktop machines suffer obsolescence in three years. Most software packages are hopelessly outmoded in about the same number of years, and the rate of change in Internet software is counted in only months.

Organizations today must accommodate to the speed of change or simply disappear as more nimble challengers provide services and products that incorporate desired innovations. Thus, leadership must be ever ready to recognize and mobilize the organization to meet change.

What has come with the electronics of a global community is a more diverse community. Beliefs, preferences, ethnicity, gender, age, physical condition, and appearances can no longer be categorized by such simple distinctions as blue-collar and white-collar workers, or management and secretarial, or professional and nonprofessional. An organization diverse yet united by purpose is far more capable and creative than one characterized by homogeneity. Using diversity as strength will not come easily for some people and some organizations. Numerous groups in the society have faced exclusions and limits on access and participation for generations. Moreover, while the culture has developed a veneer of tolerance and equality, fundamental divisions and disparities exist below the surface. Conflicts because of diversity must be expected to arise, but the successful organization will view conflicts as opportunities for greater understanding. Effective leadership in the new paradigm will not be leadership that accommodates or simply recognizes diversity. Successful leadership will use diversity for the creativity and strength it offers to the organization.

Transforming Traditional Organizations into Self-reflective and Thinking Organizations

Change, competition, and global forces are the new environment of all organizations today. Neither public nor private entities can successfully erect barriers or tariffs to shield themselves from such processes. Moreover, as more work becomes knowledge work, jobs and wealth flow to those regions of the globe with the conditions that most favor knowledge work.

To change from an organization built around an assembly line model to one that fosters awareness, learning, and creativity is to change the organization's culture. Hierarchy, proof of effort, means of rewards, job location, and tools must change. Assembly line organizations must change or they will cease to exist. In the private sector, assembly line work is simply being exported to low-cost-labor countries. There it will have a few more years of existence until technological advances eliminate the need for the high labor content. Since exporting public work to another country is not likely, privatization will be used to transfer the function out of the public sector. Once in the private sector, the conversion will occur.

Moving traditional bureaucratic organizations to self-reflective, thinking organizations requires vision, trust, data, and repeated experiences of learning. All members of the organization must come to understand the common purpose of the organization, and individual striving at all levels must come from pride in one's work, not from fear of supervision.

Creating New Organizations

The model organizations of the twentieth century were large-scale entities with dozens, even hundreds, of layers of supervision. Substantial organizational resources were placed in creating specialized jobs and control procedures to try to keep everyone marching in the direction dictated from the top. The value of the employee was how well the person followed orders, not how thoughtful, creative, or independent he or she was. Uniformity of direction with command from the top, compliant employees, and large-scale organization designs are now more pictures of the past than patterns for the future. The organizations that are rising to replace the old are

organizations that are responsive to a changing environment,
able to create new products and services based upon changes in demand and resources,
not based only in one physical location, and
able to restructure themselves as need and circumstances require.

Such organizations revise the relationships between the organization and the employee that grew out of the mass production era. In that era, the definition of the product or service came from the top and then separate roles were divided out among the workers. These new organizations depend upon the workers—especially work teams—to define the service or product, including how it will be created and delivered. With high levels of environmental change and vigorous competition for resources, these new organizations are dependent upon very special people. These are employees who have a strong commitment to the organization and are dedicated to continuous improvement and innovation. Much of the entrepreneurial activity of the last two decades has resulted in many more organizations created along the lines of the new paradigm.

Different Psychological Relationships between the Individual and the Organization

In the scientific management model much of the relationship between the employer and the worker was similar to that between a parent and a young child. The employer knew what was best for the worker and established the work and working conditions. Employees whose performance met the expectations of the employer would receive payment and continuing work. Those who did not were corrected (punished); if their behavior did not change, they would be banished from the workplace (fired). Such conditions tended to reward compliant behavior and actually promoted psychological helplessness. Since rewards flowed from following directions, when a new or novel situation occurred, workers tended to do nothing until told what to do.

Such psychological orientations are anathema to thinking organizations. Turbulent and competitive environments continuously produce novel challenges, and successful organizations must have members who can invent rather than wait for new direction.

Decision Making under Each Model

How decisions are made and why they are made define the organizational model. Typical decision-making patterns for traditional organizations and the new organization are shown in Table 5.

Thus, how decisions are made becomes a ready clue to the type of model used in organizing work.

Some General Characteristics of Organizations under the New Paradigm

We have learned these things to date from our work with public and private organizations that are becoming thinking organizations.

Table 5. Decision-making Models

Decision Model	Characteristics
Craft	Performed through the expertise of the artisan and the acceptance of the purchaser.
Scientific Management	The responsibility of management and in limited spheres of the foreman; decision making held at the top and passed or delegated to lower levels.
Human Relations	Allocation of a level of participation to workers; participation seen as a means of getting more worker cooperation.
Thinking Organization	Consensus; seen as the method to secure quality.

There is a clear understanding among all organization members about the vision, goals, and processes of the organization. This is in clear contrast to older models of organization where persons are isolated from other persons and one division may have little understanding of another division.

There is energy and conflict within the organization, but the conflict is not between persons or competing camps. The conflict is over ideas and attempts to improve progress toward goals. Fear, political correctness, and political connectedness are insignificant themes.

The existence of hierarchy is subtle and there is little emphasis on titles, offices, and dress. Leaders are known by their inspirational qualities and their abilities to encourage work, not by the fear or awe they invoke. Leadership is visible at all levels at a personal level.

There is an emphasis on democratic participation and consensus. However, there is simultaneously a strong push toward and even conflict upon reaching high levels of performance. Excellence is demanded. Everyone is expected to contribute and no one is permitted to "opt out."

Decisions are made in a "data-rich" atmosphere. Internal data, surveys, and focus groups are continuously used. External data on customers and clients are eagerly sought, as are data on similar and even very different organizations.

There is a pride and understanding of the uniqueness of the organization. Traditions exist, are known, and revered. While information is readily gathered about other organizations, there is not an attempt to simply apply solutions coming from other entities. Rather, solutions from others are taken apart and then carefully examined for potential application in the organization. The organization knows "what its knitting is and sticks to it."

There is a readiness for risky and bold undertakings but little time for quick and utopian solutions. Improvement and advancement are seen as an ongoing responsibility. Somehow the pride in tradition and a sense that unexpected challenges can occur at any time remain in functional balance. The organization is neither staid nor rife with anxiety. Rather than being driven by anticipation and control, the organization focuses on resiliency and adaptation. It is assumed that much of the future cannot be adequately anticipated, much less controlled. Consequently, the organization prepares for the future by being resilient and ready to use serendipity as it occurs. Where centralized organizations seek to control the future and are often cautious, these new organizations feel that being prepared for the unexpected is the effective strategy.

By assuming that the future will present surprises, the organization places a premium upon developing networks of partnerships. Networks increase the likelihood that talent will be available to exploit opportunities. Moreover, the use of networks lessens the likelihood that the organization will have its resources locked into divisions that may become obsolete. It is far easier to break a partnership than to close a division.[4]

There is great enthusiasm for work and pride in accomplishments. People do not just put in 8-to-5 hours but view their work as part of their life; they take pride in showing the workplace to friends and family and explaining what they do. Clearly, work accomplishment is part of how the people define themselves to others at home and in the community.

Office dress and "dress down" Fridays have little importance. Dress and appearance are governed by the tasks at hand, and the importance of the work, not appearances, drives conduct.

The organization of the work is typically through teams and the work itself drives how the offices are laid out. Teams are the focus point for standards, values, and the way problems are solved.

Crises Coming with the Paradigm Shift

Paradigms change when the dominant paradigm fails to handle problems or provide an adequate framework to address issues. Moreover, when one part of a culture experiences a change in its dominant paradigm, that change can trigger change in other institutions and create new paradigms there as well. When the physics of Copernicus moved the center of the universe from the Earth and made our planet only one of several planets orbiting a star, the consequences went far beyond a more adequate cosmology or solar astronomy. The social order of the Middle Ages, much of which dated to antiquity, trembled and then collapsed. Royalty, the aristocracy, and the Roman Catholic Church were shaken to their foundations by this paradigm change, leaving little of western culture untouched.

The scope of change that is underway today may prove to have consequences as complete and as far-flung as the Copernican Revolution or the transition from agrarianism to industrialization. It is impossible to predict all the ramifications that come from large-scale paradigm change. In all cases, both positive and negative consequences flow. The following are two of the visible consequences that come from the current change.

The Inadequacy of Knowledge Work as the Source of Employment

A fundamental problem that lies within the inevitable move to knowledge work is how available work will be for all who want it or need it. Because of the new global markets for labor and the move to modes of manufacturing and construction that minimize labor, the prospects in the United States for unskilled and semiskilled labor are bleak.[5]

From the Second World War until today, the percentage of employees working in services has increased from less than half of the labor force to approximately 70 percent. While 35 million new jobs were created from 1973 to 1989, approximately half of these were very low-skilled jobs with probable starting salaries at or below the minimum wage. Bluestone and Harrison have described the changing nature of jobs in America as "deindustrialization," with higher-paying industrial jobs being lost for lower-paying service jobs.[6] Indeed, Robert Reich has argued that much of the new face of poverty today in the nation is that of families with at least one employed member, but with wages so low that the family remains in poverty.[7] The problem is most acute in the country's urban areas, where a subculture or underclass seems to be developing. There unemployment is the rule, with few remaining middle- or upper-class families. Such prosperous families have long left the city for suburban neighborhoods; businesses that generate jobs and attract capital as well as successful role models for younger persons are rare. Minorities are disproportionately caught in these inner cities, and part of the change in the neighborhoods reflects a change in the composition of families. To these neighborhoods the term "feminization of poverty" has come to be applied.[8] In such neighborhoods as many as one half of all families may be headed by a single adult, a woman, and usually the family suffers substantial poverty. Poverty, along with a lack of role models, seems to increase the likelihood of violent crime and youth gangs.

Moreover, because of the rapid rate of social and technological change, the status of the middle class is not secure. At risk are the long-term prospects for even individuals with higher levels of education but without the skills or motivation for continuous learning. One of the major surprises of the application of information technologies has been the lessened need for managerial positions as well as general labor. Much of management activity is simply assigning work, then aggregating information from workers and passing the information to higher levels. However, computer networks and smart agents in databases can readily do many of these tasks. Thus as organizations become more information and technology rich, there is less need for middle managers. As technology pushes workers and leaders closer, managers become superfluous.

A critical problem faced by the work to build a new paradigm is how to accord status, dignity, and the fundamentals of existence when jobs may be so limited in number and so demanding of unusual talent. Such conditions may mean that vast numbers of the population may not be able to hold jobs.

Despite its many shortcomings, the assembly line model produced an expansion of jobs that served as mechanisms to distribute the wealth generated by the model. While the transition to a new paradigm is in an early stage, the inequitable distribution of employment with the monetary and psychological benefits that derive from employment is a growing problem. Age, lack of education, and physical and mental handicaps are a greater burden in a less generous society. Chronic unemployment, homelessness, youth violence, out-of-wedlock pregnancies, and other social ills can be resolved only through a social compact, not through the expectation that individuals are always able to solve their own problems. The social compact of the industrial era was built upon sizable income streams that generated tax revenues to provide governmental services, volunteerism, and philanthropy, which became mechanisms to meet such human needs. Some comparable mechanism has yet to surface in this new paradigm.

The Coming Focus on the Public Sector

Until the late 1980s, it seemed that public service organizations such as government, regulatory bodies, and educational institutions were immune from these gales of creative destruction coursing through the business world. These public entities are the parts of the society and the economy that are less creatures of open markets and more expressions of limited monopolies. However, restless public and legislative interests have begun to apply the same metaphors of lean structure, demands for continuous improvement, quick responsiveness, consumer-orientation, visible effectiveness, and quality to the public sector.

This restlessness and the subsequent changes result in tangible dislocations among many groups in the society. Ominously, some sectors of the society seem inclined to lash out at public institutions or otherwise identify governmental entities as their enemy and tormentor. Movements—some violent, others manifesting themselves in sharp turns in voting preference—are now appearing across the country that challenge the authenticity and integrity of public institutions. Congress is seeing unmatched rates in this century of members choosing not to return, and public ratings of government and government services are alarmingly negative. Threats by citizen groups against legal structures are becoming as common and as frequent as were the conflicts of the 1960s. Concerns about the viability of essential public services such as crime protection, public health care, elementary and secondary education, and Social Security are suggestive of how critical times have become.

The crisis demands that we secure the same sense of urgency and dedication in reinventing the public organization as is now underway in private sectors. It is under such conditions of pressure and open challenge that public institutions must now examine what the new challenges and metaphors mean for them.

Creating the New Paradigm in the Public Sector

Nothing less than a new paradigm is called for to replace the old approaches in government. Government, like older industrial organizations, has been constructed during this century in a specialized and hierarchical model. The German sociologist Max Weber, in laying the foundation for modern bureaucratic theory, described government structures in modern societies as having a permanent and enduring aspect, though political leaders will come and go. The idea of functions, such as enforcing traffic rules, and positions, such as police officer, provided a permanency to public institutions with individuals hired to fulfill those functions and in time replaced by other hirings. The structure of the organization became the permanent feature; individual occupants were transitory role players. Individual civil servants were prized if they were anonymous and treated all persons equally. Yet the other side of the coin of treating everyone the same is treating people impersonally. For large-scale government to function smoothly, it must follow the dictum of impersonality. Yet it is this impersonality as well as the size of scale and permanence that is now the threat to civic life.

The history of technology, the presence of social conflict, and the imperatives of mass scale in businesses and governments have shaped representative government. For example, when letters moved by horse and travel consisted of barges on waterways or carriages on unpaved roads, a distance of thirty miles might require a day's time. A seat of government a hundred miles distant, much less a thousand, simply precluded much direct citizen involvement. Thus, the intimate quality of town hall government and direct democracy in New England villages was modified to representative government. Since physical distances prevented everyone from participation, a representative form was substituted. Participation, particularly at a distance and with representatives, enhanced the importance of literacy. Being able to read and write were thus conditions of participation. Thus, literacy was a crucial element in securing the right to vote, and voting was restricted by degrees to those advantaged by literacy. From the beginning, part of the original narrowness of the franchise of full and equal citizenship in America was the inability of many groups in the society to be able to read and secure education. Such denials of participation are part of the history of the development of representative government.

Lastly, understanding government has seemed with the passage of time to require specialists and has resulted in two semipermanent classes of persons in the governing process: the elected official and the career civil service employee. Certainly, this is part of the reason why government, as originally intended as a process of participation and inclusion, has come to resemble the complex hierarchical organizations of the commercial world.

Yet participation, commitment, and dedication are at least as important to civic affairs as they are to commercial efforts to build a better laptop computer, automobile, or copying machine. In essence, the public sector must secure the same conditions with its members that corporate America seeks to secure in its pursuit of quality.

The Role of Data

Information is the spur for change. During much of this century, both our public and private institutions enjoyed high levels of success. The problem with success is that we become "world-closed." Our efforts become our own standards and set us up to be blindsided by a competitor. The more we see only one part of what we do and the more our work keeps us from contact outside of the organization, the more we are at risk for adverse change.

Without the mechanisms of the market, which permit alternatives and benchmarks, public entities must develop other or additional structures to measure quality and maintain continuous improvement. Part of becoming more oriented to quality is becoming more sensitive to available data. Inherent in the socialization of the assembly line model is a high level of concentration on the task at hand and a tendency to become "world-closed" rather than "world-open." Having a variety of data available and learning to be open to the data are necessary ingredients in socializing members of the organization to the "outside world."

Importing Quality Concepts

Mostly the "quality movement" (TQM and the like) comes from outside of the public sector, as did the paradigm of specialization and control of scientific management.[9] Yet clearly one of the major themes in the public sector today is the growing concern about quality and attempts to apply principles from the quality movement to public sector organizations. However, the extension of a metaphor from one kind of an organization to another organization may be fraught with difficulties. The appearance of the quality movement may be more than just the need for a management adjustment. It may indeed be a caution to examine how all organizations relate to people both inside and outside the organization. It can also be a challenge to civic responsibility and the integrity of public institutions. If the quality movement represents all these things, then the answer must be a great deal more than simply borrowing some tools from companies that produce quality products.

Important Issues in Creating a Quality Paradigm for Civic Obligations

When there are free markets and genuine competitors, an organization has ready benchmarks to compare its products and services with what other organizations offer. When there is not a competitor, capable organizations will seek other means to find ways to benchmark. In some cases, an organization may simply compare a function in the organization to a like function handled in a different organization. How quickly and effectively telephone inquiries are handled is a simple but highly useful benchmarking activity. All organizations should continuously survey customers as part of the process of acquiring external data. However, it is very important to carefully consider who the customers are. For a fast food outlet, the answer is simple: the person at the counter or the drive-through window is an important part of the customer equation.

There is reason to assume that when open markets exist, and viable and bona fide competitors are present, such conditions will support products of higher quality and a process of continuous improvement. This is clearly happening in the private sector. Such conditions are less likely to occur in the public sector and may not always be desirable. Some public sectors, such as institutions of higher education, appear to benefit in terms of quality by the fact that there are alternative suppliers and some competition between providers. There is at least reason to suspect that an extension of the model to secondary and primary education might improve both the quality of education provided and the level of citizen support for the institution. On the other hand, some public functions do not seem readily transferable to the marketplace. For example, should there be alternative courts where a potential litigant, plaintiff, or offender might shop around for better quality? Should one have the choice of alternative state departments and select the one that best represents one's personal view of other countries and quickness in issuing passports? Since one's residence is an accident of geography, should a person be permitted, with ready access to powerful communication tools, to shop around for the city, county, and state of one's choice? In a way, wealthy people and corporations already do that by choosing which geographical setting is their domicile.

Should such government entities become part of a more fluid market for all citizens? Simply pursuing a cure of creating market mechanisms is not a fully adequate answer for securing public confidence.

Consider public or governmental organizations, which provide more of a challenge in determining who the customer is. Correctional programs provide an apt example. The criminal justice system and correctional facilities are extraordinarily large entities in today's society. In 1995 over one million persons were in jails and prisons and three million additional persons were supervised in community corrections. The cost of operating the system is over $70 billion per year. Now, for a correctional system, who is the customer?

The offender?

The person victimized by the offender?

The police officer and prosecutor who apprehended and convicted the offender and expect the offender either to cease being a problem or to be kept from the community?

The court that sentenced the offender?

The family of the offender that hopes the offender will be returned to the family as a resource, not a drain on the family?

The community that demands that the community be safe from the offender?

The legislature or the governor that funds and directs the correctional enterprise?

The local community, employee families, and local businesses that are supported by the economic dimension that the correctional entity represents in the community?

In reality, all of these are the customers of the correctional system. The challenge to the correctional system is, first, to understand that all are legitimate customers and, second, to develop services and responses to effectively deal with all of these customers.

Universities provide another rich example of how complex and important the customer dimensions are to understanding and improving quality. Like the correctional system, higher education is one of the larger service entities in our society and the question "who is the customer?" is complex. The current student body is both a customer and a product of the university. Undergraduate and graduate students are two very different kinds of customers. Undergraduates are often customers not just of the classroom but also of housing and food services. Graduates are customers that typically require far more "custom work" than the undergraduates. Conducting research, developing a thesis, and creating an original work require far greater levels of one-to-one assistance. Graduate schools and professional schools are customers of the undergraduate program. Undergraduate programs can stand or fall to the extent they are successful in getting their graduates accepted by graduate programs. Parents are customers, and as any dean of students can attest, what a parent expects is often at some variance from what a freshman or sophomore expects. Taxpayers, legislators, federal granting agencies, wealthy benefactors, accrediting entities, foundations, and employers are also important customers, as are the alumni. As any university president knows, varsity athletics is a critical product to some very discerning and influential customers for every university. Indeed, in some institutions when athletic facilities are compared to classrooms and laboratories, scholarship, teaching, and learning seem incidental university missions.

Summary

What appears to be underway in American life is a great shift in the paradigms of how social life should be organized. The pursuit of quality and the desirability and inevitability of change have been reasserted as major themes in civic dialogue. Paradigms are not theories or concepts. They are rather frameworks within which theories and concepts come into being. Paradigms include values, assumptions about what reality is and what activities are both sensible and appropriate.[10]

Typically, the power and ubiquity of a paradigm are such that it pervades thoughts, actions, and processes so thoroughly that a person does not realize that perceived reality is mediated by the paradigm. The major paradigm—the assembly line method with its attendant attributes of mass scale, volume production, specialization, and control—is waning as a belief in how best to order life. The manufacture of things, like the growing of crops, no longer occupies even a large minority of the workforce. The definition of work moves on to other things, other tasks. What is underway is a dynamic yet contentious process of creating a paradigm that gives meaning to life. It is a paradigm that successfully furthers progress toward the most salient problems of the time and provides order from the growing chaos and lack of meaning that accompanies the demise of an older and now less viable paradigm.

Amid this swirling sea of change, is there also the need for organizations that do not change but have the responsibility of preserving core values? The rationality of markets and capitalism is to continuously perfect a match of product to customer demand that produces the greatest profits. In an open system, then participating organizations will continuously change. But is there a need for some organizations that keep time to a different clock? Entities that serve as a repository of knowledge, values, and findings must judiciously consider calls for change. Courts must reflect contemporary issues but must also maintain fidelity to core values.

Which organizations will survive through this process and what new ones will come into existence are impossible to forecast. It is clear, though, that the changes will be sharp, and for most organizations there will be stumbles and a longing to return to the more hierarchical and rigid formulas of the old paradigm.

The opportunity to participate in creating a new paradigm is an exciting prospect, yet daunting in the range of consequences that it implies. For the public sector, it means establishing structures that respond to multiple customers or clients. It means thinking very thoroughly about services to determine exactly what each service is, what the measurable consequence of the service is, and what the most appropriate organizational vehicle for providing the service is. It requires undertaking a deep reassessment of the relations among organizations, members of organizations, and the community.

One of the most laudable principles of the quality movement is the imperative to completely understand all of the processes necessary to produce a given good or service. Increases in the quality of education, justice, public health, medicine, transportation, and law enforcement —all the functions of the public sector and dimensions of community life—can come only from applying this principle fully. The greatest contribution of the quality movement could be the full and vigorous application of this principle to domains other than manufacturing. The results of such a movement could well end the malaise that seems endemic to much of civic life and services and renew the quest for perfection in public life that is so central to the American experiment.

We have now come full circle in this book, as we started with a concern about how we can increase the sense of ownership and comity between citizens and the organizations that citizens create. Much of what was lost to the individual and the community during the years of the ascendancy of the scientific management paradigm was the loss of power over organizations. Now we see that for organizations to survive, that power must be returned to the members of the organization.

This will in turn help to restore civility, reciprocity, and "belonging-ness" to the community.

The SOE and its processes are an example, one part of the steps necessary to create the new paradigm. Our data on this tool extend for several years yet are restricted largely to Texas state agencies. Moreover, much of the data on explicit organizational change comes in slowly as organizational change is usually a process taking years rather than days. Yet available data suggest that important and useful changes are occurring.

For any organization using tools such as the survey described in this book, a latent benefit is likely to be the positive gains for the community. The SOE emphasizes equality in the organization and mutual responsibility in improving quality. Returning the survey data is an exercise in shared and collective responsibility in defining and solving problems. These steps emphasize horizontal and reciprocal obligations and responsibilities. The use of the SOE and the efforts to return the data and involve leadership and employees in promoting excellence serve to restore a sense of both competency and dignity to bureaucratic work. These actions provide a model for how people should relate to each other both inside the organization and to people outside the organization. The SOE process thus serves as a model for personal responsibility, pursuit of understanding, honesty, trust, commitment, and good civic conduct.

Appendix A
Survey of Organizational Excellence

See following page.

Survey of Organizational Excellence

Many demographic questions are included in this survey for research purposes. To ensure your responses remain anonymous, employing organizations will **not** receive reports for categories that contain less than 5 people.

ORGANIZATION CODES

To complete the following three items refer to the insert that is included with this questionnaire.

1. [ ] [ ] [ ]
2. [ ] [ ] [ ]
3. [ ] [ ] [ ]

(Ovals 0-9 for each column)

MARKING INSTRUCTIONS
- Use number 2 pencil only.
- Make dark marks that fill the oval completely.
- Erase cleanly any mark you wish to change.
- Make no stray marks.

USE A NO. 2 PENCIL ONLY

CORRECT MARK ●

My sex
○ Male
○ Female

My employment status in the organization
○ Regular   ○ Temporary

Hours per week employed
○ 40 or more hours
○ 21 - 39 hours
○ less than 21 hours

I am currently in a supervisory role.
○ Yes   ○ No

I received a promotion during the last two years.
○ Yes ○ No

My race/ethnic identification
○ African-American
○ Hispanic-American
○ Anglo-American
○ Asian-American or Pacific Islander or Native American Indian
○ Other

My age
○ Under 20 years
○ 20 - 29 years
○ 30 - 39 years
○ 40 - 49 years
○ 50 - 59 years
○ 60 years and older

I received a merit increase during the last two years.
○ Yes   ○ No

There is more than one wage earner in my household.
○ Yes   ○ No

I am the primary wage earner in my household.
○ Yes   ○ No

I plan to be working for this organization in two years.
○ Yes   ○ No

I grew up in
○ Texas
○ The Northeast
  (ME, NH, VT, MA, RI, CT, PA, NY, DE, MD, NJ, DC)
○ The Southeast
  (VA, WV, KY, TN, NC, SC, FL, GA, AL, MS, LA, AR)
○ The Southwest (OK, NM, AZ, CA, NV, UT, CO)
○ The Northwest (WA, OR, ID, MT, WY)
○ The Midwest
  (ND, SD, NE, KS, MO, IA, IL, WI, IN, OH, MI, MN)
○ Alaska or Hawaii
○ Other

The number of persons in my household including myself is:
○ 1 person
○ 2 persons
○ 3 persons
○ 4 persons
○ 5 persons
○ 6 persons
○ 7 persons or more

My length of service with this organization
○ Under 1 year
○ 1 - 2 years
○ 3 - 5 years
○ 6 - 10 years
○ 11 - 15 years
○ Over 15 years

I have lived in Texas
○ Less than 2 years
○ 2 - 10 years
○ Over 10 years

The zip code where I live is

EXAMPLE
| 7 | 5 | 0 | 2 | 9 |

(Ovals 0-9 for each column)

My highest educational level is
○ did not finish high school
○ high school diploma (or GED)
○ some college
○ Associate degree
○ Bachelor's degree
○ Graduate degree

My annual gross (before taxes) salary
○ Less than $11,000
○ $11,001 - $15,000
○ $15,001 - $19,000
○ $19,001 - $23,000
○ $23,001 - $27,000
○ $27,001 - $31,000
○ $31,001 - $35,000
○ $35,001 - $39,000
○ $39,001 - $43,000
○ $43,001 - $47,000
○ $47,001 - $51,000
○ $51,001 - $55,000
○ $55,001 - $59,000
○ $59,001 - $63,000
○ $63,001 - $67,000
○ Over $67,000

© School of Social Work, The University of Texas at Austin, 1997

127181

160

On the following statements, please indicate how strongly you agree or disagree that the statement describes your **organization as a whole**. The strength of your response can range from **strongly disagree (SD)** to **strongly agree (SA)**. If you do not have any information about a particular statement or the statement is not applicable to you, indicate that by **bubble (NA)**. You will be asked about your perceptions of your immediate work group in another section of the survey.

DON'T KNOW/NOT APPLICABLE
STRONGLY AGREE
AGREE
FEEL NEUTRAL
DISAGREE
STRONGLY DISAGREE

- We are known for our customer service.
- We are constantly improving our services.
- Our goals are consistently met or exceeded.
- We produce high-quality work that has a low rate of error.
- We know who our customers are.
- We develop services to match our customers' needs.
- Average work is rewarded the same as excellent work.
- My close contacts and co-workers are a lot different from people elsewhere in the organization.
- Every employee is valued.
- Managers are committed to incorporating cultural diversity.
- Employees have adequate computer resources (hardware and software).
- Computerized information is easily shared among divisions in this organization.
- Computerized information is shared as appropriate with other organizations.
- The right information gets to the right people at the right time.
- Information and knowledge are shared openly in this organization.
- This organization integrates information and acts intelligently upon that information.
- The work atmosphere encourages open and honest communication.
- Employees feel that they must always go through channels to get their work done.
- We routinely use different people from different parts of the organization to solve problems.
- Work groups (that group of people with whom you have daily contact) are trained to incorporate the opinions of each member.
- Work groups receive adequate feedback that helps improve their performance.
- We work well with other organizations.
- We work well with our governing bodies (the legislature, the board, etc.).
- We work well with the public.
- We understand the state, local, national, and global economic issues that impact this organization.
- Employees have an opportunity to participate in the process of strategic planning and goal setting.
- Employees know how their work impacts other employees in the organization.
- Decision making and control are given to employees doing the actual work.
- Employees seem to be working toward the same goals.
- There is a basic trust among employees and management.
- Each employee is given the opportunity to be a leader.
- Employees feel a sense of pride when they tell people that they work for this organization.
- Work in this organization feels like it is "coming together."
- We are efficient.
- Employee productivity is high.
- We "walk our talk."
- Employees feel that their efforts count.
- "The buck stops here" describes how employees accept personal accountability.
- Employees have adequate resources to do their job.
- Employees are given accurate feedback about their performance.
- Alternative work schedules (flex-time, compressed work weeks, job sharing) are offered to employees.
- Training is made available to employees in personal growth and development.
- Training is made available to employees so that they can do their job better.
- Employees have access to information about job opportunities, conferences, workshops and training.
- Management knows whether an individual employee's life goals are compatible with organizational goals.
- Employees feel safe working in this organization.
- Employees feel that they work in pleasant surroundings.
- There is a feeling of community within this organization.

All responses are confidential

Please continue on the next page

■ ■ Page 2   Mark Reflex® by NCS MM217044-1   654321   ED99   Printed in U.S.A.

161

Marking instructions for this section:

On the following statements, please indicate how strongly you agree or disagree that the statement describes your **organization as a whole**. The strength of your response can range from **strongly disagree (SD)** to **strongly agree (SA)**. If you do not have any information about a particular statement or the statement is not applicable to you, indicate that by **bubble (NA)**. You will be asked about your perceptions of your immediate work group in another section of the survey.

DON'T KNOW/NOT APPLICABLE
STRONGLY AGREE
AGREE
FEEL NEUTRAL
DISAGREE
STRONGLY DISAGREE

The environment supports a balance between work and personal life. ⓈⒹ Ⓓ Ⓝ Ⓐ ⓈⒶ Ⓝ

The pace of the work in this organization enables employees to enjoy their work. ⓈⒹ Ⓓ Ⓝ Ⓐ ⓈⒶ Ⓝ

New ideas suggested by employees are seriously considered for implementation. ⓈⒹ Ⓓ Ⓝ Ⓐ ⓈⒶ Ⓝ

Employees balance their focus on both the long range and short term. ⓈⒹ Ⓓ Ⓝ Ⓐ ⓈⒶ Ⓝ

Creativity and innovation in work are encouraged. ⓈⒹ Ⓓ Ⓝ Ⓐ ⓈⒶ Ⓝ

People who challenge the status quo are valued. ⓈⒹ Ⓓ Ⓝ Ⓐ ⓈⒶ Ⓝ

Promotion recommendations are made by a team of evaluators. ⓈⒹ Ⓓ Ⓝ Ⓐ ⓈⒶ Ⓝ

Raises and promotions are designed to ensure that workers are rewarded solely for their performance. ⓈⒹ Ⓓ Ⓝ Ⓐ ⓈⒶ Ⓝ

Salaries are competitive with similar jobs in the community. ⓈⒹ Ⓓ Ⓝ Ⓐ ⓈⒶ Ⓝ

Benefits can be selected to meet individual needs. ⓈⒹ Ⓓ Ⓝ Ⓐ ⓈⒶ Ⓝ

Information about benefits and policies is adequate and understandable. ⓈⒹ Ⓓ Ⓝ Ⓐ ⓈⒶ Ⓝ

Benefits are comparable to those offered in other jobs. ⓈⒹ Ⓓ Ⓝ Ⓐ ⓈⒶ Ⓝ

The overall benefits and compensation packages offered by my employer were a consideration for me to take this position. ⓈⒹ Ⓓ Ⓝ Ⓐ ⓈⒶ Ⓝ

The benefits and compensation packages were adequately explained to me when I was hired. ⓈⒹ Ⓓ Ⓝ Ⓐ ⓈⒶ Ⓝ

Changes in benefits and compensation packages have been explained to me during the last two years. ⓈⒹ Ⓓ Ⓝ Ⓐ ⓈⒶ Ⓝ

I fully understand my health insurance and disability plan. ⓈⒹ Ⓓ Ⓝ Ⓐ ⓈⒶ Ⓝ

I fully understand my retirement plan. ⓈⒹ Ⓓ Ⓝ Ⓐ ⓈⒶ Ⓝ

Our employees are generally ethical in the workplace. ⓈⒹ Ⓓ Ⓝ Ⓐ ⓈⒶ Ⓝ

I am confident that any ethics violation I report will be properly handled. ⓈⒹ Ⓓ Ⓝ Ⓐ ⓈⒶ Ⓝ

Sexual harassment is not tolerated in this organization. ⓈⒹ Ⓓ Ⓝ Ⓐ ⓈⒶ Ⓝ

Diversity is valued in this organization. ⓈⒹ Ⓓ Ⓝ Ⓐ ⓈⒶ Ⓝ

I am satisfied with the continuing education/training opportunities offered by my employer. ⓈⒹ Ⓓ Ⓝ Ⓐ ⓈⒶ Ⓝ

I am satisfied with the medical insurance benefit offered by my employer. ⓈⒹ Ⓓ Ⓝ Ⓐ ⓈⒶ Ⓝ

I am satisfied with the sick leave benefit offered by my employer. ⓈⒹ Ⓓ Ⓝ Ⓐ ⓈⒶ Ⓝ

I am satisfied with the vacation benefit offered by my employer. ⓈⒹ Ⓓ Ⓝ Ⓐ ⓈⒶ Ⓝ

I am satisfied with the retirement benefit offered by my employer. ⓈⒹ Ⓓ Ⓝ Ⓐ ⓈⒶ Ⓝ

I am satisfied with the dental insurance benefit offered by my employer. ⓈⒹ Ⓓ Ⓝ Ⓐ ⓈⒶ Ⓝ

I am satisfied with the vision insurance benefit offered by my employer. ⓈⒹ Ⓓ Ⓝ Ⓐ ⓈⒶ Ⓝ

I am satisfied with the holiday benefit offered by my employer. ⓈⒹ Ⓓ Ⓝ Ⓐ ⓈⒶ Ⓝ

I am satisfied with the Employee Assistance Program (E.A.P) benefit offered by my employer. ⓈⒹ Ⓓ Ⓝ Ⓐ ⓈⒶ Ⓝ

Marking instructions for this section:

On the following statements, please indicate how strongly you agree or disagree that the statement describes your **immediate work group**. The strength of your response can range from **strongly disagree (SD)** to **strongly agree (SA)**. If you do not have any information about a particular statement or the statement is not applicable to you, indicate that by **bubble (NA)**.

DON'T KNOW/NOT APPLICABLE
STRONGLY AGREE
AGREE
FEEL NEUTRAL
DISAGREE
STRONGLY DISAGREE

Employees have a strong orientation toward high performance, accuracy and honesty. ⓈⒹ Ⓓ Ⓝ Ⓐ ⓈⒶ Ⓝ

When possible, problems are solved before they become a crisis. ⓈⒹ Ⓓ Ⓝ Ⓐ ⓈⒶ Ⓝ

Members of my work group trust each other. ⓈⒹ Ⓓ Ⓝ Ⓐ ⓈⒶ Ⓝ

I feel that I can give my supervisor my opinion on work related issues without fear of getting into trouble. ⓈⒹ Ⓓ Ⓝ Ⓐ ⓈⒶ Ⓝ

Our goals are consistently met or exceeded. ⓈⒹ Ⓓ Ⓝ Ⓐ ⓈⒶ Ⓝ

Employees are involved in decision-making. ⓈⒹ Ⓓ Ⓝ Ⓐ ⓈⒶ Ⓝ

My work group is kept informed about how the organization is doing in achieving its goals and plans. ⓈⒹ Ⓓ Ⓝ Ⓐ ⓈⒶ Ⓝ

There is a feeling of community within my work group. ⓈⒹ Ⓓ Ⓝ Ⓐ ⓈⒶ Ⓝ

We are known for our customer service. ⓈⒹ Ⓓ Ⓝ Ⓐ ⓈⒶ Ⓝ

Every employee is valued. ⓈⒹ Ⓓ Ⓝ Ⓐ ⓈⒶ Ⓝ

Employees in my work group have adequate computer resources (hardware and software). ⓈⒹ Ⓓ Ⓝ Ⓐ ⓈⒶ Ⓝ

Our work group receives adequate feedback which helps improve our performance. ⓈⒹ Ⓓ Ⓝ Ⓐ ⓈⒶ Ⓝ

Employees are given accurate feedback about their own performance. ⓈⒹ Ⓓ Ⓝ Ⓐ ⓈⒶ Ⓝ

All responses are confidential   *Please continue on the next page*

Marking instructions for this section:

On the following questions, consider how your organization has changed during the last two years. Read each statement and assess how your organization compares now to two years ago. Your response can range from **1 (the organization is doing much worse)** to **5 (the organization is doing much better)**. If you do not have any information about a particular statement or the statement is not applicable to you, indicate that by **bubble (NA).**

DON'T KNOW/NOT APPLICABLE
THE ORGANIZATION IS PERFORMING MUCH BETTER
THE ORGANIZATION IS PERFORMING BETTER
THE ORGANIZATION IS IS THE SAME AS IT WAS TWO YEARS AGO
THE ORGANIZATION IS PERFORMING WORSE
THE ORGANIZATION IS PERFORMING MUCH WORSE

Assess the quality of the service that this organization provides to its customers.	① ② ③ ④ ⑤ NA
Assess the appreciation shown by this organization for the diversity of its employees and customers.	① ② ③ ④ ⑤ NA
Assess the quality of communication among employees within this organization.	① ② ③ ④ ⑤ NA
Assess the effectiveness of work groups.	① ② ③ ④ ⑤ NA
Assess the overall satisfaction with benefits and compensation.	① ② ③ ④ ⑤ NA
Assess the opportunity for employee training and development.	① ② ③ ④ ⑤ NA
Assess whether the resources and facilities are adequate for employees to do their jobs.	① ② ③ ④ ⑤ NA
Assess the level of stress and burnout that is experienced in this organization.	① ② ③ ④ ⑤ NA
Assess the creativity and innovation in this organization.	① ② ③ ④ ⑤ NA
Assess how well the organization works with other organizations.	① ② ③ ④ ⑤ NA
Assess the response time and efficiency of work produced in this organization.	① ② ③ ④ ⑤ NA
Assess the overall effectiveness of this organization.	① ② ③ ④ ⑤ NA
Assess the commitment shown by employees in this organization.	① ② ③ ④ ⑤ NA
Assess whether paperwork is in balance with other responsibilities.	① ② ③ ④ ⑤ NA
Assess whether the resources available to this organization are matched to the workload.	① ② ③ ④ ⑤ NA
Assess the level of empowerment of employees.	① ② ③ ④ ⑤ NA
Assess the level of bureaucracy in this organization.	① ② ③ ④ ⑤ NA

Marking instructions for this section:

Please read the following statements and fill in the bubble corresponding to the response which most clearly reflects your personal feelings.

In general how would you say that decisions are made.

- ○ Policy is made completely at the top.
- ○ Policy is made mostly at the top.
- ○ Broad policy is made at the top with delegation.
- ○ Policy is made throughout the organization.
- ○ It is difficult to determine how policy is made.
- ○ Policy is mostly imposed from the outside.

How free do people feel to talk to their supervisors about their job?

- ○ Not at all.
- ○ Rarely and with caution.
- ○ Sometimes.
- ○ Most of the time.
- ○ Almost all of the time.
- ○ All of the time.

Marking instructions for this section:

Your organization may have requested that you answer some additional questions. The questions appear on the insert that is included with this questionnaire. Please read each of the questions and fill in your responses in the spaces below. Please skip this section if your insert does not include additional questions.

Question 1 ① ② ③ ④ ⑤ ⑥	Question 6 ① ② ③ ④ ⑤ ⑥	Question 11 ① ② ③ ④ ⑤ ⑥	Question 16 ① ② ③ ④ ⑤ ⑥
Question 2 ① ② ③ ④ ⑤ ⑥	Question 7 ① ② ③ ④ ⑤ ⑥	Question 12 ① ② ③ ④ ⑤ ⑥	Question 17 ① ② ③ ④ ⑤ ⑥
Question 3 ① ② ③ ④ ⑤ ⑥	Question 8 ① ② ③ ④ ⑤ ⑥	Question 13 ① ② ③ ④ ⑤ ⑥	Question 18 ① ② ③ ④ ⑤ ⑥
Question 4 ① ② ③ ④ ⑤ ⑥	Question 9 ① ② ③ ④ ⑤ ⑥	Question 14 ① ② ③ ④ ⑤ ⑥	Question 19 ① ② ③ ④ ⑤ ⑥
Question 5 ① ② ③ ④ ⑤ ⑥	Question 10 ① ② ③ ④ ⑤ ⑥	Question 15 ① ② ③ ④ ⑤ ⑥	Question 20 ① ② ③ ④ ⑤ ⑥

All responses are confidential   ***THANK YOU FOR YOUR PARTICIPATION !***

■○■■○○■■○○○○■■■■○○○○○○○   127181

163

Examples of Custom Questions and Use of Additional Demographic Options

Custom Questions

I can disagree with my supervisor without fear of getting in trouble.
   1. strongly disagree 2. disagree 3. neutral 4. agree 5. strongly agree 6. don't know/not applicable

Overall, the agency has improved since it was reorganized in 19__.
   1. strongly disagree 2. disagree 3. neutral 4. agree 5. strongly agree 6. don't know/not applicable

I have attended the agency's quality initiative training.
   1. yes 2. no

Problems in my work group are solved before they become a crisis.
   1. strongly disagree 2. disagree 3. neutral 4. agree 5. strongly agree 6. don't know/not applicable

Travel policies are understandable.
   1. strongly disagree 2. disagree 3. neutral 4. agree 5. strongly agree 6. don't know/not applicable

Employees in my immediate work group are concerned about making ethical decisions about their work.
   1. strongly disagree 2. disagree 3. neutral 4. agree 5. strongly agree 6. don't know/not applicable

Employees in this organization, outside of my work group, are concerned about making ethical decisions about their work.
   1. strongly disagree 2. disagree 3. neutral 4. agree 5. strongly agree 6. don't know/not applicable

I understand the mission of this organization.
   1. strongly disagree 2. disagree 3. neutral 4. agree 5. strongly agree 6. don't know/not applicable

The employee newsletter helps me understand how other employees' work contributes to this organization.
   1. strongly disagree 2. disagree 3. neutral 4. agree 5. strongly agree 6. don't know/not applicable

Employees know what sexual harassment is and is not.
   1. strongly disagree 2. disagree 3. neutral 4. agree 5. strongly agree 6. don't know/not applicable

Individuals with alternative lifestyles are treated the same as other employees in my work group.
   1. strongly disagree 2. disagree 3. neutral 4. agree 5. strongly agree 6. don't know/not applicable

Diversity is a part of the agency's overall culture.
   1. strongly disagree 2. disagree 3. neutral 4. agree 5. strongly agree 6. don't know/not applicable

Services to our external customers have improved as a result of the agency's quality training initiative.
   1. strongly disagree 2. disagree 3. neutral 4. agree 5. strongly agree 6. don't know/not applicable

Services to our internal customers have improved as a result of the agency's quality training initiative.
   1. strongly disagree 2. disagree 3. neutral 4. agree 5. strongly agree 6. don't know/not applicable

Demographic Options

1. Please indicate your assigned region:

Code   *Region*

001   Austin (not Central Office Staff)
002   Dallas
003   Fort Worth
004   Houston

005   Lubbock
006   Central Office Staff (Austin)

2. Please indicate your job function category:

Code   *Job Function*

001   Administrative Technician
002   Investigator
003   Staff Supervisor, Manager, Director
004   Attorney, Legal Assistant, Legal Secretary
005   Support Staff: Accounting, Budget Analyst, MIS,
        Human Resources
006   Planner
007   Other

3. Please indicate your program area:

Code   *Program Area*

001   Licensing
002   Investigations
003   Client Support
004   Research
005   Technical Support
006   Other

4. Please assess the amount of time you typically spend in direct interactions with the organization's external customers.

Code   *Estimate of Time*

001   On a typical workday, I interact with external customers most of the day.
002   On a typical workday, I interact with external customers about 50% of the day.
003   On a typical workday, I interact with external customers about 25% of the day.
004   On a typical workday, I rarely or never interact with external customers.

Appendix C
Survey Checklists

Survey Checklist 1 – Establish the Overall Plan with Executive Staff

❑ 1. Review Survey data with executive staff.

❑ 2. Assess the rate of response.

❑ 3. Identify the most salient strengths and weaknesses as reported by the Survey by sorting out the highest and lowest questions.

❑ 4. Benchmark the organization's scores by comparing them to statewide scores and other available comparison groupings.

❑ 5. Develop plans for circulating all the data sequentially and provide interpretations for all staff. Do this with 3 to 4 weekly or monthly reports or organization newsletters. Report a portion of the Constructs and Questions, providing the data along with illustrations pertinent to the given organization.

❑ 6. Designate the Change Team.

❑ 7. Identify the Work Unit Groups to ensure all employees get an opportunity to see and review the data. Replicate *Steps 2, 3, 4*, and *8* within each Work Unit Group.

❑ 8. Establish Procedures for recording the deliberations of the Work Unit Group and returning those data to the Change Team so that the Team can decide upon the Top Priority Change Topic and Methods necessary for making the change.

Survey Checklist 2 – Assess the Response Rate

What is the 1998 response rate?	RATE:

Low response levels suggest that the organization has high levels of alienation, indifference or suspicion. Building trust and reducing defensive compliant behavior is the first order of business for organizations with low response rates.

Is the 1998 response rate lower than the 1996 response rate?	☐ Yes	☐ No

Response rates that are decreasing from previous levels on earlier administrations suggest growing problems of compliance or alienation and/or problems with survey administration.

Is the 1998 response rate lower than the statewide response rate?	☐ Yes	☐ No

The statewide response rate provides an appropriate benchmark to assess your organization's response.

Is the 1998 response rate lower than the comparison group response rate?	☐ Yes	☐ No

Several comparison groups are available including organizations of similar size and mission. It is often helpful to use a variety of benchmarks.

Does the Survey respondent pool reflect the demographic make-up of the organization?	☐ Yes	☐ No

Look particularly at any groups that may not be responding. These questions may not be relevant to some groups of employees or they may be areas of controversy and defensiveness. Employee unwillingness to respond is a critical indicator of highly contentious issues. Such areas may be marked for longer-term efforts to secure improvement. Questions with relatively high standard deviations represent areas of disagreement. Postpone tackling these questions until reasons for disagreement are understood.

Survey Checklist 3 – Identify the Most Salient Strengths and Weaknesses and Benchmark Them

Step One
Identify two of the highest scoring and two of the lowest scoring Constructs.

High

Construct No.	Construct Name	1998 Score	1996 Score*	Statewide Score

Low

Construct No.	Construct Name	1998 Score	1996 Score*	Statewide Score

*if available

Step Two
Examine the specific questions that produce the Constructs. For details see Chapter 4.

High 1:

Q No.	Score	Question Text

High2

Q No.	Score	Question Text

Low 1:

Q No.	Score	Question Text

Low 2:

Q No.	Score	Question Text

Survey Checklist 4– Designate the Change Team

Names

Executive Staff Member	
Member 1	
Member 2	
Member 3	
Member 4	
Member 5	
Member 6	
Member 7	
Member 8	

Survey Checklist 5– Work Unit Groups

Step One

Select a time to have <u>every employee</u> participate in a work unit group to review the reports as they are distributed to all staff, with one group leader assigned to every group. The size of the groups should be limited to about a dozen people at a time. A time limit should be set not to exceed two hours.

Step Two

Build the groups around actual organizational work units and start each meeting by reviewing strengths as indicated in the data report. Brainstorm on how to best address weaknesses.

Names of Work Group Members

Survey Checklist 6– Report on Top Priority Change Topic

List the topic for Top Priority Change and describe methods for addressing the item. Return this form from each Work Unit Group to the Change Team.

Top One or Two Topics for Change

Suggested Methods

Appendix D
Survey Customers

Organization	Executive Director	Survey Liaison
Department of Criminal Justice	Wayne Scott	Carol B. Jones
Department of Mental Health and Mental Retardation	Don Gilbert	Morris Arnold, Vickie Helms
Department of Human Services	Eric M. Bost	Penny Potter
Department of Transportation	William G. Burnett	Sara Barker
Department of Public Safety	Dudley Thomas	Eliseo de Leon
Department of Protective and Regulatory Services	Jim Hine	Sally Periard
Department of Health	William R. Archer III	Jeannie Weaver
Workforce Commission	Mike Sheridan	Krista Julian
Youth Commission	Steve Robinson	Eric Young, Kelly Mason
Natural Resources Conservation Commission	Dan Pearson	Lan Hartsock
Parks and Wildlife Department	Andrew Sansom	Annette Dominguez, Landy Johnston

(*continued*)

Organization	Executive Director	Survey Liaison
Rehabilitation Commission	Vernon M. Arrell	Mike Mericle
Workers' Compensation Commission	Bob Marquette	Gilda Garcia
Department of Insurance	Elton Bomer	Ann Cook
Education Agency	Mike Moses	Adam Jones
General Services Commission	Tom Treadway	Melda Benavidez
Commission for the Blind	Pat D. Westbrook	Robert Counts
Alcoholic Beverage Commission	Doyne Bailey	Rolando Garza
Teacher Retirement System	Charles L. Dunlap	Kathy Brandner
Lottery Commission	Lawrence E. Littwin	Nancy Goodman-Gill
Water Development Board	Craig Pedersen	Earline Baker
Higher Education Coordinating Board	Don Brown	Mary E. Smith
State Auditor's Office	Lawrence Alwin	Mark Pope
Public Utility Commission	Brenda Jenkins	Beth Phillips
Commission on Alcohol and Drug Abuse	Terry Bleier	Donzie Burnett
Department of Economic Development	Brenda Arnett	Michael Jones
Library and Archives Commission	Robert S. Martin	Vanessa H. Siordia
Department of Banking	Catherine A. Ghiglieri	Randall S. James
Commission on Fire Protection	Gary L. Warren	Barbara Jenkins

Organization	Executive Director	Survey Liaison
Office of Administrative Hearings	Shelia Bailey Taylor	Amy Hodgins
Historical Commission	Curtis Tunnell	Nina Chamness
Lamar University Institute of Technology	Robert D. Krienke	Robert D. Krienke
Department of Information Resources	Carolyn Purcell	Larry Zeplin
Real Estate Commission	Brian Francis	Brian Francis
Interagency Council on Early Childhood Intervention	Mary Ockerman Elder	Carmelita Cabello
Board of Nurse Examiners	Kathy Thomas	Mark W. Majek
Juvenile Probation Commission	Vicki Spriggs	Glenn Neal
Board of Pharmacy	Gay Dodson	Cathy Stella
Commission on Law Enforcement Officer Standards and Education	D. C. Jim Dozier	Jayne Tune
Department on Aging	Mary Sapp	Aimee Mick
Cosmetology Commission	Delores L. Alspaugh	Penny Black
Credit Union Department	Harold E. Feeney	Lynette Pool-Harris
Board of Registration for Professional Engineers	John R. Speed	John R. Speed
Board of Vocational Nurse Examiners	Marjorie A. Bronk	Linda Rae Kent
Texas Board of Architectural Examiners	Cathy L. Hendricks	Cathy L. Hendricks

(continued)

Organization	Executive Director	Survey Liaison
Savings and Loan Department	James L. Pledger	James L. Pledger
Low-Level Radioactive Waste Disposal Authority	Lawrence R. Jacobi, Jr.	Rita Hodde
Board of Examiners of Psychologists	Sherry Lee	Brian L. Creath
Cancer Council	Emily Untermeyer	Emily Untermeyer
Incentive and Productivity Commission	M. Elaine Powell	Dan Contreras
Optometry Board	Lois Ewald	Lois Ewald
Texas State Board for Educator Certification	Mark Littleton	Mark Littleton
University of Texas Applied Research Laboratories	Dr. Michael Pestorius	Kathy Kaderka
University of Missouri at Columbia	Michael Kelly	Michael Kelly
Southeast Missouri State University	Paul Keys	Paul Keys
Missouri Office of Family Services	Peggy Torno	Peggy Torno
Eglin Air Force Base	Harold Keeson	Harold Keeson
Cal Farley Boys and Girls Home	Mary Reeve	Mary Reeve
West Texas Rehabilitation Center	Tracy McHaney	Tracy McHaney
General Libraries, UT-Austin	Harold Billings	Jo Anne Hawkins, Peggy Mueller
Human Resources, UT-Austin	Sandra Haire	Kay Franklin
Dana Center, UT-Austin	Uri Treisman	Rose Asera

Organization	Executive Director	Survey Liaison
College of Engineering, UT-Austin	Ben Streetman	Neal Armstrong
University of Texas Performing Arts Center	David Deming	Warren C. Whittaker

Notes

1. History and Development of the Survey of Organizational Excellence

1. F. J. Roethlisberger and W. J. Dickson, *Management and the Worker.*
2. M. P. Follett, *Creative Experience;* M. P. Follett, *Dynamic Administration;* M. Sherif and C. Sherif, *An Outline of Social Psychology.*
3. The state and characteristics of the rivalry are the subject of the August 1997 issue of *Forbes ASAP.* An assessment in that issue emphasizes the role of culture as the explanation of innovation and prosperity and suggests that northern California is increasingly ahead of the East Coast and certainly Austin.
4. Sharp has issued a number of studies calling for a leaner, more focused structure in state government. Reports include *Disturbing the Peace, Gaining Ground, Against the Grain,* and *Breaking the Mold.* These and other reports are available from the Texas State Comptroller in Austin or through that agency's Web site at www.window.texas.gov/tpr/tpr.html.
5. The tools and findings presented here have applicability to all organizations—public or private as well as federal, state, or local. Because of the nature of their franchise in the culture, private organizations are often more likely to be early adopters of change and have often been highly influential in bringing organizational orientations to public entities. Chapters 7 and 8 examine this phenomenon. The explicit tie of the SOE activity in the state of Texas is a recognition of this reality. Developing

benchmarks with nongovernmental sectors provides comparable perspectives from highly successful and competitive private organizations.

6. Beginning in 1994–1995, state agencies were directed to include SOE results or related assessments in their strategic planning documents as described in *Instructions for Preparing and Submitting Agency Strategic Plans for the Period 1997–2001*, issued by the Governor's Office of Budget and Planning and the Legislative Budget Board.

2. The Survey Concept in Organizational Development

1. The role of labor in forming industrial and postindustrial economies and states is complex and typically oppositional. See K. Coates, *The New Worker Cooperatives*, and K. Coates, *How to Win*. James K. Galbraith's *The New Industrial State* presents an American view; for a more conflictual view, see R. Hyman, *Industrial Relations*.

2. Vilfredo Pareto, *The Mind and Society*. Pareto emphasized that small areas of distribution often account for disproportionate influence. His work is often criticized for what appears to be an elitist orientation that supported the notions of Germany and Italy during the 1930s.

3. Guidelines for Understanding the SOE Data

1. Mark Yudof and Ilene J. Busch-Vishniac, "Total Quality: Myth or Management in Universities," *Change*, November/December 1996.

2. An important reference for survey design is the Total Design Method presented in M. A. Dillman, *Mail and Telephone Surveys*.

3. Suggested levels of Cronbach's statistic are discussed in D. D. Tull and D. I. Hawkins, *Marketing Research*.

4. Procedures for Organizational Assessment and Intervention

1. These five categories are selected for heuristic purposes. They provide convenient categories in which leadership can direct change efforts.

2. A large and rich literature exists in supervision.

3. Important work on team effectiveness includes the writings of the Ohio State Leadership studies and the works of Robert Blake and Jane Mouton.

4. See Michael Lauderdale, *Burnout;* C. Maslach and A. Pines, "Burnout, the Loss of Human Caring," in *Experiencing Social Psychology*, ed. Pines and Maslach; and H. J. Freudenberger, *Burnout: The High Cost of Achievement*.

5. Using the SOE in Changing the Organization

1. Arie de Geus, *The Living Company*.

2. James C. Collins and Jerry Porras, *Built to Last*. This book addresses the characteristics of American companies that remain successful over the

years. The authors identify eighteen companies that they feel are exceptional, especially through their visionary aspects.

3. Gareth Morgan uses the concept of metaphor as a complete foundation to address approaches to understanding organizations. See *Images of Organization* and "Paradigms, Metaphors, and Puzzle Solving in Organizational Theory," *Administrative Science Quarterly* 25 (1980): 605–620.

4. An influential book on how to create highly successful organizations is Tom Peters and Robert Waterman, *In Search of Excellence*. Some of the Peters and Waterman criteria of what produces excellence were not affirmed by Collins and Porras.

5. Steve H. Murdock, Md. Nazrul Hoque, Martha Michael, Steve White, and Beverly Pecotte, *Texas Challenged*, provided a lengthy assessment of demographic change in Texas and its likely consequences for state government.

6. In some cases, one simply encounters crazy people in an organization; it is important to see this as a challenge. John Bruhn is an earlier observer of this challenge and offers cogent recommendations. See John G. Bruhn, "Managing Crazy Behavior in Organizations," *Health Care Supervision* 16, no. 3 (1998): 17–25.

6. Some Results from Organizations Using the SOE

1. Some scholars have argued that rational change cannot readily occur in the public sector. Charles Perrow, *Complex Organizations*, presents the argument in the strongest form. Somewhat earlier, in *Social Theory and Social Structure*, Robert Merton anticipated—with his distinction of the manifest and latent functions of organizations and change—that rationality was not always readily achieved.

2. How markets operate and should operate is a domain of study far beyond the scope of this book. Markets and currencies have long experienced government intervention, efforts by producers and consumers to regulate markets, and disruptions caused by natural and social events. If there are a number of independent producers or sellers, and if there are sovereign consumers who can freely choose among the sellers, then we can expect quality to increase and prices to decline. In many areas of product and service, we do not have independent producers and sovereign consumers, so other means are needed to provide competition and comparison.

3. Among the largest and best-known consumer ratings are those of the nonprofit Consumers Union. Many general and special-purpose magazines rate products. The prices of used automobiles are tracked by rating services, and the J. D. Powers organization is known for its annual ratings of automobile quality.

4. Several comparative publications are now available for educational institutions and professional schools. *U.S. News and World Report* provides an annual evaluation. Peterson's publishes ratings of various educational

entities. Consumers Union has periodic but irregular reviews of costs and some comparative information.

5. We often request the Texas Poll to provide data from a statewide panel of citizens to compare with the SOE data on certain questions. The Texas Poll is a joint effort of the College of Communications and Harte-Hanks Communications. Poll data are collected several times a year.

6. Successful organizational change does not guarantee continuity of the organization or leadership. The Texas Real Estate Commission received several new board members shortly after Bill Kuntz and Brian Francis were hired in 1995. The chair, a new board member, apparently decided early in his tenure that he wanted different leadership for the agency. In the spring of 1997 the board replaced Bill with Brian as the acting executive director and initiated a search for a new executive director. Bill is now no longer with the agency; yet many of the efforts begun under his leadership continue.

7. Figures are from the 1997 Texas Legislative Appropriations Act and the Legislative Budget Board.

7. How the Pursuit of Quality Undermines the Mass Production/Bureaucratic Model

1. The production process was highly personal and idiosyncratic to each artisan. The uniqueness was expressed through the variation of form and design from craftsman to craftsman. Personal trademarks or signatures that a craftsman would place on an item emphasized the role of the individual. Goods or services of extraordinary high value were associated with a given craftsman. Such trademarks, like the painter's signature, were intended to ensure the purchaser of the authenticity and thus the quality of the article. Indeed, the corporate logos of today (Mercedes Benz's three-pointed star, McDonald's golden arches, Apple's apple logo, Nike's swoosh insignia, Microsoft's Windows flying window) are echoes of the craftsman's trademarks of antiquity.

   In the typical production routine the craftsman would purchase raw materials and then through the application of his craft create an item for the trade. To a limited degree, the craftsman might produce a small inventory of items, but given the scarcity of capital and the nature of the creative process, most items were produced only when a purchaser came forth. Then only with a sale in hand would the craftsman make the product. Thus, production was closely tailored to the needs of each customer. Part of this production process was a closeness, an intimacy, among craftsman, the article created, and the purchaser.

2. Henry Ford is used as an illustration of the hundreds of examples that can be drawn from the literature on the development of the industrial state. Alfred Sloan Jr. of the General Motors Corporation produced the more complete and powerful example of the industrialized automotive plant.

3. Robert Kanigel, *The One Best Way*. This highly detailed biography covers the patrician birth of Taylor, his experiences as a factory worker in the early factories of the eastern United States during the late nineteenth century, and his rise to being perhaps the most influential management theorist and propagandist in this century.

4. The creation of a middle class of employees and consumers was not a simple, smooth evolution from family farms and sharecropping. The pull of factory jobs was so strong in some countries that agricultural production was threatened for lack of field labor. In the factories whole families were pressed into employment and the use of child labor and sweatshops became common. Enlightened ownership, unions, and government all played important roles in seeing that the wealth that came from the new ways of making things was not simply concentrated in the hands of a few.

5. During much of this century labor and management relations in the United States were at a standoff. The role of the "birth print" of early events is important in the history of individuals, organizations, and cultures. An important factor to keep in mind when there is an attempt to bring about change in an organization is that change is not simply drawing a new organization on a blank slate. Every organization has its own culture as well as the culture that each employee brings to the organization. Often events that occur early in an organization provide a pattern—what Stinchcombe, in "Social Structure and Organizations," called a birth print—that may well carry forward for many years. The birth print patterns that were created in the early years of the Ford Motor Company illustrate part of that company's culture and a major pattern of management and labor relations during the years of hegemony of the assembly line model.

6. In one way, the war had been designed and fought by the concepts of assembly line management with top-down control from the Pentagon and the White House. Much of the best of American technology was brought to bear on the effort. The effort sought to extend the control right down to small fighting units in the jungles of Southeast Asia. Systems concepts such as "villages controlled" and "body counts" were utilized to make the endeavor discrete, measurable, and controllable.

7. Masaaki Imai, *KAIZEN*; Kaoru Ishikawa, *What Is Total Quality Control?*

8. So telling in the experience with automobiles and electronics was the fact that the American economy no longer enjoyed the world domination that it had experienced since the end of World War II. American companies found that they faced scrappy competitors everywhere in the world. Moreover, the domestic economy was being invaded from abroad by tough, resourceful, inventive businesses that sought to fully displace American companies. These conditions began to spark alarm in corporate boardrooms, union leadership, political parties, and academia. Soon it became clear that this competition was going to be very difficult. Not only did many of the foreign companies have lower labor costs, but they also

had the kind of workers and organizations that seemed to confer clear advantages to the foreign companies.

9. W. E. Deming, *Out of Crisis.*

10. Joseph M. Juran, *Juran on Planning for Quality;* Joseph M. Juran, "Made in U.S.A.: A Renaissance of Quality," *Harvard Business Review,* July 1993.

11. American Telephone and Telegraph and two of its components, its manufacturing arm, Western Electric (particularly the Chicago factory called the Hawthorne plant), and the research and development facility, Bell Laboratories, played a disproportionate role in contributing leaders and concepts to organizational theory in this century. It is important to remember that during much of this period, American Telephone and Telegraph was a national monopoly free of competition in its markets and, compared with the telephone systems of other nations, phenomenally successful in the quality and dependability of its telephone service and in the creative contributions of its researchers in Bell Laboratories.

12. P. Crosby, *Quality Is Free.*

8. Creating the New Paradigm: Thinking Organizations

1. Andrew Grove, one of the leaders of Intel, uses the phrase "only the paranoid survive." Intel does not wait to satisfy the customer but has a strategy of using innovation to beat competition. Microsoft uses a similar strategy of recognizing and purchasing superior products. The entire development of the personal computer from the Altair to the Internet is an example of technology leading customer needs, not simply satisfying them. In each of these examples the technology came before the need and desire of the customer. The development of object-oriented programming, networking, and graphical user interfaces from the Palo Alto Research Park of Xerox all represent cases of innovation running far ahead of customer preferences and needs.

2. Kevin Freiberg and Jackie Freiberg, *NUTS!* This is a highly readable account of how Herb Kelleher broke with dozens of airline traditions and built an enormously successful service organization.

3. George L. Kelling and Catherine M. Coles, *Fixing Broken Windows.* The criminal justice system has begun to recognize the severe problems associated with the hierarchical and specialized approach to dealing with crime and violence. Kelling and Coles chronicle the shift to a far different organization form for the police.

4. Aaron B. Wildavsky, *Searching for Safety.* Wildavsky provides a clear contrast between two different assumptions of the future (knowable or unknowable) and the strategies that are driven by each.

5. D. S. Eitzen and M. B. Zinn, *In Conflict and Order.* The book provides extensive commentary about that idea that the United States is in the last stages of industrialization and the factors that are causing change.

6. B. Bluestone and B. Harrison, *The Deindustrialization of America.*

7. Robert B. Reich, "Who Is Them?" *Harvard Business Review* 69, no. 2 (March 1991): 77–89. Reich, Harvard lecturer and former secretary of labor, is known for his advocacy for a national labor policy to address the growing problems of low-wage and low-benefit jobs. The article focuses on the growth of a class of full-time workers with wages so low that, in spite of their employment, they remain in poverty.

8. W. J. Wilson, *The Truly Disadvantaged*, discusses gangs in inner cities and even higher rates of female-headed households.

  U.S. Census, Bureau of the Census, *1990 Census, Summary Tape, File 3C*, provides estimates of the number of female-headed households in urban areas. P. E. Zopf, Jr., *American Women in Poverty*, provides a detailed examination of how poverty is disproportionally distributed by gender—the feminization of poverty. See also T. Duster, "Crime, Youth Employment, and the Underclass," *Crime and Delinquency* 33 (1987): 300–316.

  J. W. Moore, *Homeboys*, uses the term "segmented labor market" to refer to those jobs that do not offer benefits, retirement, higher wages, or the prospect of higher wages and job security.

9. Substantial efforts have now been underway for more than a decade to bring these concepts to the public sector as well as to service work in general. See E. Berman, "Implementing TQM in State Welfare Agencies," *Administration in Social Work* 19, no. 1 (1995); Leonard L. Berry, *On Great Service*; M. E. Weiner, *Human Services Management*; D. Hubbard, *Continuous Quality Improvement*; R. Lewis and D. Smith, *Total Quality in Higher Education*; L. Sheer and D. Teeter, *Total Quality in Higher Education*; and S. T. Moore and M. J. Kelly, "Quality Now: Moving Human Services Organizations toward a Consumer Orientation to Service Quality," *Social Work* 41, no. 1 (January 1996).

10. Thomas S. Kuhn, *The Structure of Scientific Revolutions*, 2d ed. Kuhn likens the change of paradigms to a revolution. He suggests that the worldview differences are so profound between two separate paradigms that meaning in one is incomprehensible in the other. Thus, paradigmatic thinking is both epistemological (how we know what we know) and ontological (what the true meaning of existence is).

Bibliography

Adams, J. D., ed. *Understanding and Managing Stress.* San Diego, Calif.: University Associates, 1980.

Argyris, Chris. *Interpersonal Competence and Organizational Effectiveness.* Homewood, Ill.: Dorsey Press, 1962.

———. *Knowledge for Action.* San Francisco: Jossey-Bass, 1993.

Berger, P., B. Berger, and H. Kellner. *The Homeless Mind.* New York: Viking Books, 1974.

Berman, E. "Implementing TQM in State Welfare Agencies." *Administration in Social Work* 19, no. 1 (1995): 55–72.

Berry, Leonard L. *On Great Service: A Framework for Action.* New York: Free Press, 1995.

Blake, R., and J. Mouton. *The Managerial Grid.* Houston: Gulf Publishing, 1970.

Bloch, M. *Feudal Society.* Chicago: University of Chicago Press, 1961.

Bluestone, B., and B. Harrison. *The Deindustrialization of America.* New York: Basic Books, 1982.

Brady, R. H. "MBO Goes to Work in the Public Sector." *Harvard Business Review* 51, no. 2 (April 1973): 75–83.

Braverman, H. *Labor and Monopoly Capital.* New York: Monthly Review Press, 1974.

Bruhn, John G. "Managing Crazy Behavior in Organizations." *Health Care Supervision* 16, no. 3 (1998): 17–25.

————. "Relevance of Health Behavior Research to Training and Practice in the Health Professions." In *Handbook of Health Behavior Research IV: Relevance for Professionals and Issues for the Future,* ed. Davis S. Gochman. New York: Plenum Press, 1997.

Carroll, S. J., and H. L. Tosi. *Management by Objectives.* New York: Macmillan, 1973.

Champy, J. *Reengineering Management.* New York: Harper, 1995.

Clegg, S. *The Theory of Power and Organization.* London: Routledge & Kegan Paul, 1979.

Coates, K. *How to Win.* Nottingham, England: Spokesman Books, 1981.

————. *The New Worker Cooperatives.* Nottingham, England: Spokesman Books, 1978.

Collins, James C., and Jerry I. Porras. *Built to Last.* New York: Harper Collins, 1994.

Connellan, Thomas K. *Inside the Magic Kingdom: Seven Keys to Disney's Success.* Austin, Tex.: Bard Press, 1997.

Crosby, P. *Quality Is Free.* New York: McGraw-Hill, 1979.

de Geus, Arie. *The Living Company: Habits for Survival in a Turbulent Business Environment.* Boston: Harvard Business School, 1997.

Deming, W. E. *Out of Crisis.* Cambridge: Massachusetts Institute of Technology, Center for Advanced Engineering Study, 1986.

Dillman, M. A. *Mail and Telephone Surveys: The Total Design Method.* New York: John Wiley and Sons, 1978.

Duster, T. "Crime, Youth Employment, and the Underclass." *Crime and Delinquency* 33 (1987): 300–316.

Eitzen, D. S., and M. B. Zinn. *In Conflict and Order.* 6th ed. Boston; Allyn and Bacon, 1993.

Edelwich, J. A., and A. Brodsky. *Burnout: Stages of Disillusionment in the Helping Professions.* New York: Human Sciences Press, 1980.

Etzioni, Amitai. *A Comparative Analysis of Complex Organizations.* New York: Free Press, 1975.

Follett, M. P. *Creative Experience.* New York: Longmans, Green, 1924.

————. *Dynamic Administration: The Collected Papers of Mary Parker Follett.* New York: Harper & Row, 1940.

Freiberg, Kevin, and Jackie Freiberg. *NUTS! Southwest Airlines' Crazy Recipe for Business and Personal Success.* Austin, Tex.: Bard Press, 1996.

Freudenberger, H. J. *Burnout: The High Cost of Achievement.* Garden City, N.J.: Anchor Press, 1980.

Frost, P. J., V. F. Mitchell, and W. R. Nord, eds. *Managerial Reality.* New York: Harper-Collins, 1995.

Galbraith, James K. *The New Industrial State.* Boston: Houghton Mifflin, 1967.

Garvin, David. "Quality Policies, Problems, and Attitudes in the U.S. and Japan: An Exploratory Study." *Academy of Management Journal* 29, no. 4 (1986): 653–673.

Garvin, David A. *Managing Quality: The Strategic and Competitive Edge.* New York: Free Press, 1988.

George, C. S. *The History of Management Thought.* Englewood Cliffs, N.J.: Prentice Hall, 1972.

Gilbreth, Frank. *Motion Study.* New York: Van Nostrand, 1911.

Gitlow, Howard S., and Shelly J. Gitlow. *The Deming Guide to Quality and Competitive Position.* Englewood Cliffs, N.J.: Prentice Hall, 1987.

Goffman, E. *Asylums.* New York: Doubleday, 1961.

Habermas, Jurgen. *Knowledge and Human Interests.* Boston: Beacon Press, 1971.

———. *Legitimation Crisis.* Boston: Beacon Press, 1975.

Hammer, M., and J. Champy. *Reengineering the Corporation.* New York: Harper, 1993.

Hegel, G. W. F. *The Logic of Hegel.* London: Clarendon, 1892.

Hersey, P., and K. H. Blanchard. *Management of Organizational Behavior: Utilizing Human Resources.* Englewood Cliffs, N.J.: Prentice-Hall, 1988.

Herzberg, F. *Work and the Nature of Man.* Cleveland: World Publishing, 1966.

Hubbard, D. *Continuous Quality Improvement: Making the Transition to Education.* Marysville, Ohio: Prescott Publishing Company, 1993.

Huizinga, J. *The Waning of the Middle Ages.* New York: Anchor Press, Doubleday, 1954.

Hyman, R. *Industrial Relations: A Marxist Introduction.* London: Macmillan, 1975.

Imai, Masaaki. *KAIZEN: The Key to Japan's Competitive Success.* New York: Random House, 1986.

Ishikawa, Kaoru. *What Is Total Quality Control? The Japanese Way.* Translated by David J. Lu. Englewood Cliffs, N.J.: Prentice-Hall, 1985.

Juran, Joseph M. *Juran on Planning for Quality.* New York: Free Press, 1988.

———. "Made in U.S.A.: A Renaissance of Quality." *Harvard Business Review* 71, no. 4 (July 1993): 42–53.

Kakar, S. *Frederick Taylor: A Study in Personality and Innovation.* Cambridge, Mass.: MIT Press, 1970.

Kanigel, Robert. *The One Best Way: Frederick Winslow Taylor and the Enigma of Efficiency.* New York: Viking, 1997.

Kanter, Rosabeth. *The Change Masters.* New York: Simon and Schuster, 1983.

Kelling, George L., and Catherine M. Coles. *Fixing Broken Windows.* New York: Free Press, 1996.

Kuhn, Thomas S. *The Structure of Scientific Revolutions.* 2d ed. Chicago: University of Chicago Press, 1970.

Lasch, Christopher. *The Culture of Narcissism.* New York: W. W. Norton, 1978.

Lauderdale, Michael. *Burnout.* San Diego, Calif.: University Associates, 1982.

Lewin, K. *Resolving Social Conflicts: Selected Papers on Group Dynamics.* New York: Harper & Row, 1948.

Lewis, R., and D. Smith. *Total Quality in Higher Education.* Minneapolis: St. Lucie Press, 1994.

Likert, R. *The Human Organization.* New York: McGraw-Hill, 1961.

McClelland, D. C. *Motivating Economic Achievement.* New York: Free Press, 1971.

McGregor, D. *The Human Side of Enterprise.* New York: McGraw-Hill, 1960.

Mantoux, P. *The Industrial Revolution in the Eighteenth Century.* New York: Harper & Row, 1962.

March, J. G., and H. A. Simon. *Organizations.* New York: John Wiley, 1958.

Marx, Karl. *Early Writings.* Harmondsworth, England: Penguin, 1975.

Maslach, C., and A. Pines. "Burnout, the Loss of Human Caring." In *Experiencing Social Psychology,* ed. A. Pines and C. Maslach. New York: Random House, 1979.

Maslow, A. *Eupsychian Management.* Homewood, Ill.: Richard D. Irwin and the Dorsey Press, 1965.

———. *Motivation and Personality.* New York: Harper & Row, 1952.

Mayo, E. *The Social Problems of an Industrial Civilization.* Cambridge, Mass.: Harvard University Press, 1945.

Merton, Robert. *Social Theory and Social Structure.* New York: Free Press, 1968.

Mintzberg, H. "Managing Government, Governing Management." *Harvard Business Review* 74, no. 3 (May–June 1996): 75–83.

Moore, J. W. *Homeboys: Gangs, Drugs, and Prisons in the Barrio of Los Angeles.* Philadelphia: Temple University Press, 1978.

Moore, S. T., and M. J. Kelly. "Quality Now: Moving Human Services Organizations toward a Consumer Orientation to Service Quality." *Social Work* 41, no. 1 (January 1996): 33–40.

Morgan, Gareth. *Images of Organization.* 2d ed. Thousand Oaks, Calif.: Sage, 1997.

———. "Paradigms, Metaphors, and Puzzle Solving in Organizational Theory." *Administrative Science Quarterly* 25 (1980): 605–620.

Murdock, Steve H., Md. Nazrul Hoque, Martha Michael, Steve White, and Beverly Pecotte. *Texas Challenged: The Implications of Population Change for Public Service Demand in Texas.* Austin: Texas Legislative Council, 1996.

Odiorne, George. *Management by Objectives.* New York: Pittman, 1965.

Pareto, Vilfredo. *The Mind and Society.* New York: Harcourt Brace Jovanovich, 1935.

Perrow, Charles. *Complex Organizations: A Critical Essay.* New York: Random House, 1979.

———. "Demystifying Organizations." In *The Management of Human Services,* ed. R. C. Sarri and Y. Hasenfeld. New York: Columbia University Press, 1978.

Peters, Tom, and Robert Waterman. *In Search of Excellence.* New York: Harper and Row, 1982.

Polanyi, K. *The Great Transformation.* New York: Holt, Rinehart and Winston, 1944.

Pines, A., and E. Aronson. *Burnout: From Tedium to Personal Growth.* New York: Free Press, 1980.

Pirenne, H. *Medieval Cities.* New York: Doubleday, 1956.

Popper, Karl. *The Open Society and Its Enemies.* Princeton, N.J.: Princeton University Press, 1963.

―――. *The Poverty of Historicism.* New York: Basic Books, 1960.

Postrel, Virginia I. "Resilience vs. Anticipation." *Forbes ASAP,* August 1997. <www.forbes.com/asap/97/0825/056.htm>

Reich, Robert B. "Who Is Them?" *Harvard Business Review* 69, no. 2 (March 1991): 77–89.

Ritzer, G. *The McDonaldization of Society.* Newbury Park, Calif.: Sage, 1996.

Roethlisberger, F. J., and W. J. Dickson. *Management and the Worker.* Cambridge, Mass.: Harvard University Press, 1939.

Rule, James B. *Insight and Social Betterment.* New York: Oxford, 1978.

Ryan, Kathleen D., and Daniel K. Oestreich. *Driving Fear Out of the Workplace.* San Francisco: Jossey-Bass, 1991.

Schorr, Lisbeth B. *Common Purpose.* New York: Doubleday, 1997.

Schumpeter, J. *Can Capitalism Survive?* New York: Harper & Row, 1978.

Senge, Peter. *The Fifth Discipline: The Art and Practice of the Learning Organization.* New York: Doubleday, 1991.

Selye, H. *Stress without Distress.* New York: Lippincott, 1974.

Seymour, Daniel T. *On Q: Causing Quality in Higher Education.* New York: Macmillan, 1989.

Sheer, L., and D. Teeter. *Total Quality in Higher Education: Case Studies in Total Quality Management.* San Francisco: Jossey-Bass, 1993.

Sherif, M., and C. Sherif. *An Outline of Social Psychology.* New York: Harper & Row, 1956.

Shewhart, W. A. *Economic Control of Quality of Manufactured Product.* New York: D. Van Nostrand Company, 1931.

Smith, A. *An Inquiry into the Nature and Causes of the Wealth of Nations,* ed. Edwin Cannan; introduction by Max Lern. New York: Modern Library, 1937.

Stinchcombe, A. L. "Social Structure and Organizations." In *Handbook of Organizations,* ed. J. G. March. Chicago: Rand McNally, 1965.

Sward, K. *The Legend of Henry Ford.* New York: Rinehart, 1948.

Taylor, Frederick W. *The Principles of Scientific Management.* New York: Harper & Row, 1911.

Texas, State of. Comptroller of Public Accounts. *Against the Grain: High-Quality, Low-Cost Government for Texas.* Austin: Comptroller of Public Accounts, 1993.

―――. *Breaking the Mold: New Ways to Govern Texas.* Austin: Comptroller of Public Accounts, 1991.

191

———. *Disturbing the Peace: The Challenge of Change in Texas Government.* Austin: Comptroller of Public Accounts, 1996.

———. *Gaining Ground: Progress and Reform in State Government.* Austin: Comptroller of Public Accounts, 1994.

———. Governor's Office of Budget and Planning. *Instructions for Preparing and Submitting Agency Strategic Plans for the Period 1997–2001.* Austin: Governor's Office of Budget and Planning and Legislative Budget Board, 1995.

Tull, D. D., and D. I. Hawkins. *Marketing Research: Measurement and Method.* New York: Macmillan, 1987.

U.S. Bureau of the Census. *1990 Census, Summary Tape, File 3C.* Washington, D.C.: U.S. Government Printing Office, 1990.

Wallerstein, I. *The Modern World-System.* New York: Academic Press, 1974.

Walton, Mary. *Car: A Drama of the American Workplace.* New York: W. W. Norton, 1997.

Weber, M. *The Protestant Ethic and the Spirit of Capitalism.* London: Allen & Unwin, 1930.

———. *The Theory of Social and Economic Organizations.* Glencoe, Ill.: Free Press, 1947.

Weiner, M. E. *Human Services Management.* Belmont, Calif.: Wadsworth, 1990.

Wildavsky, Aaron B. *Searching for Safety.* New Brunswick, N.J.: Transaction Books, 1988.

Wilson, James Q., and George L. Keeling. "Making Neighborhoods Safe." *Atlantic Monthly,* February 1989, 46–52.

Wilson, W. J. *The Truly Disadvantaged.* Chicago: University of Chicago Press, 1987.

Woodward, J. *Industrial Organization: Theory and Practice.* New York: Oxford University Press, 1965.

Wrege, C. D., and A. G. Perroni. "Taylor's Pig-tale." *Academy of Management Journal* 17 (1974): 6–27.

Yudof, Mark, and Ilene J. Busch-Vishniac. "Total Quality: Myth or Management in Universities." *Change,* November/December 1996, pp. 19–27.

Zemke, Ron. *The Service Edge: 101 Companies That Profit from Customer Care.* New York: New American Library, 1989.

Zopf, P. E., Jr. *American Women in Poverty.* New York: Greenwood Press, 1989.

Index